GOD'S
TO ABORTION

A TRUE LOVE STORY

The story of how I went from pro-abortion to
pro-child, from pro-death to pro-life, from pro
my choice to pro-God's choice.

TAYLOR C. R. PATTERSON

A wholly owned subsidiary of TBN

God's Answer to Abortion: A True Love Story, the Story of How I Went from Pro-Abortion to Pro-Child, from Pro-Death to Pro-Life, from Pro My Choice to Pro-God's Choice

Trilogy Christian Publishers A Wholly Owned Subsidiary of Trinity Broadcasting Network

2442 Michelle Drive Tustin, CA 92780

Rights Department, 2442 Michelle Drive, Tustin, CA 92780.

Trilogy Christian Publishing/TBN and colophon are trademarks of Trinity Broadcasting Network.

For information about special discounts for bulk purchases, please contact Trilogy Christian Publishing.

Trilogy Disclaimer: The views and content expressed in this book are those of the author and may not necessarily reflect the views and doctrine of Trilogy Christian Publishing or the Trinity Broadcasting Network.

Manufactured in the United States of America

10 9 8 7 6 5 4 3 2 1

Library of Congress Cataloging-in-Publication Data is available.

ISBN: 978-1-64773-271-4

E-ISBN: 978-1-64773-272-1

"For love is strong as death" (Song of Solomon 8:6).

God can speak through the voice of a child.

Living souls never die.

DEDICATION

This book is dedicated to the following people who changed my life:

Peter Crabtree
The first to see a shining light in the dark rose known as me.

My one and only beautiful mother, the only person who ever really understood me,
Valerie Jean Green, the love of my life.
Play in paradise, Mom. God willing, I will see your beautiful face again in heaven.

My hero and dad,
James David Patterson.
Thanks for not being afraid of a terrible teenage fool and still loving me.

Three ladies at Ralphs
who loved and helped my son: Paula, Chavonna, Gilver.

And the beautiful girl from the Deli who purchased a very special birthday cake for my son.

One man who inspired the world:

"Stolen Greatness."

I once read that the "highest human act is to inspire"

Nipsey Hussle

Twitter, 2019

RIP, "Stolen Greatness" (March 31, 2019).

A late, truly heartbreaking, unexpected addition to this book, Marcus Lamb.

The man who made the poor, the needy, and undistinguished people like me feel just as special as the rich, the distinguished, and the celebrated. He made us all feel like we were a part of the family and truly loved by God.

<3

**"Faith is not just something you say;
faith is something you do."**

"God, I'll go where You want me to go; I'll do what You want me to do; I'll say what You want me to say, and I'll be what You want me to be. That's what God is looking for."

Marcus Lamb's memorial service, Daystar Television, December 7, 2021

To the family, Marcus's supernatural number is four. I believe four is the number that represents the spiritual presence of angels.

CONTENTS

FOREWORD

God knows what we don't know, sees what we don't see, hears what we don't hear, and feels what we don't feel. He knows when we are ready, even when we don't.

"God, I can't explain You to them, and even if I could, they would never believe me."

But honestly, not that any man could ever understand God.
"See, I have set before thee this day life and death, […] choose life," said Jesus Christ in Deuteronomy 30:15, 19.

Let me start by saying that this book was not written to condemn you; for to condemn you, I would first have to condemn myself. I love you all!

This book was written for three reasons:

Number one: this book is my God-given assignment. Every word in it was placed into my mind and heart by the Holy Spirit and given to me to share with you. The mission will be completed.

Number two: to inspire both men and women alike to stop aborting their children whose only mission in life was to be born.

And number three: that more souls would be saved before it is too late, as Yeshua saved me.

"Judge not and ye shall not be judged, condemn not and ye shall not be condemned" was what Yeshua said in Luke 6:37.

Dear God, Lord Jesus, Holy Spirit, and Christopher, thank you for saving my life.

Although my foolish heart would not let me save your life here on the earth, I pray my soul, spirit, and heart do not fail me so that one day I will see you again.

Love, Mom.

<3

INTRODUCTION

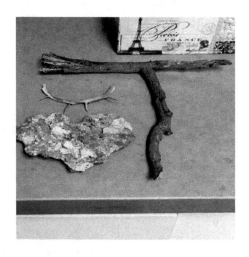

A True Story.

Actually,

a True Love Story

"God bless the beasts and the children, for in this world,
they have no voice, they have no choice"
(Carpenters, "Bless the Beasts and the Children," 1971).

<>

Thoughts...

Have you ever been hungry for love from someone, hungry for love from someone who simply didn't love you back and never would?

How did it feel?

Unrequited love is a bore, isn't it?

Better stated: it is truly painful.

"But God, they are going to think I am crazy."

The still small voice spoke and said, **"Goeth..."**

I understood this to be the voice of the Holy Spirit, saying, "Go and follow God's Word."

"He who justifies the wicked and he who condemns the righteous are both alike an abomination to the Lord" (Proverbs 17:15, ESV).

My Supernatural God-Given Assignment

A short time after the death, I started having dreams and weird experiences. It took a year or so for me to figure out the purpose and meaning of the dreams, visions, supernatural experiences, finding artifacts, wonders, messengers, and modern technology (television, movies, documentaries).

When I finally figured out what was happening to me and that God allowed Yeshua, the Holy Spirit, and angels to open the doors to heaven, hell, future appointed times, revelations, and things to come, I had an awakening to the understanding that God was giving me an assignment. I knew I needed to turn away from sin and go about the mission of fulfilling God's purpose and will for my life. I started to pay close attention to all things happening; I started making notes daily; I started writing down all the dreams (paper and pencil); I started paying closer attention to everything, every little detail, big or small. I have started looking for the signs of the Holy Spirit's presence in the next several years and for the rest of my life. However, I was not moving at the speed of light. I am not sure if this was out of fear, a busy work schedule, or if I just really wanted to make sure I got every single detail of every supernatural dream, occurrence, sighting (that's the word I created for supernatural visions of angelic shadows or translucent colors floating from one space in my home to another), wonder, experience, and supernatural physical artifact correct to ensure every detail written in this book was from the Spirit of God and not me.

Nevertheless, while contemplating my assignment, I couldn't stop thinking about the biblical story of Jonah and the whale. I knew without a shadow of a doubt that I did not want to become a Jonah. The Jonah who initially defied God's will and was swallowed up by the whale. That said, the story of Jonah stayed with me during the time I was writing this book.

At the very end of writing, revising, and editing this

book in 2021, this supernatural excerpt from the Bible appeared to me on my screen while I was scrolling through Google, looking for correct Bible citations.

Jesus said,

> This is an evil generation, it seeks a sign, and no sign will be given to it except the sign of Jonah, the prophet. For as Jonah became a sign to the Ninevites, so also the Son of Man will be to this generation.

Luke 11:29–30 (NKJV)

Honestly, I had never heard this verse before. I was never aware of the fact that Jonah was actually the sign to the Ninevites of impending doom. I found very interesting the fact that I stumbled upon this verse at the very tail end of writing and editing this book.

If you need a sign (and I sincerely hope you'll overcome this need), if you must have a sign and are still looking, maybe this book (since you selected to read it) is your sign or first message from God that will be for you to decide and further investigate through faith and love.

I Am Not a Prophet

For the record: I am not a prophet, nor would I ever profess to be, nor would I ever want to be. I am a servant of the Lord God and a disciple of Christ Jesus, Yeshua. Being a prophet is a lot of responsibility, and since God is omniscient, He is always watching. Take heed.

Some of you may ask how I knew this was my God-given assignment.

Because I would have never chosen this road for myself. The road was presented; I was led, and I followed. Hence, I answered the call to my assignment.

Like Subtle Wind, the Voice of the Holy Spirit Speaks

2020

During the writing of this book, I became a bit stagnant and reached a stalemate. When, suddenly, in 2020, I heard the voice of God, Yeshua, and the Holy Spirit say, "Finish the book this year." So, I did. Well, almost, except for the editing and final additions to the manuscript.

2021

In January of 2021, that still small voice came again and whispered, "Publish the book this year." I did not understand the reasoning, nor did I question it; I just proceeded as I was told. Later in the year, I would come to understand why I got the nudge to publish the book in this prophetic year.

"Just because we can't see it, let's not be so arrogant as to think that it doesn't exist" (Rabbi K. A. Schneider, *Discovering the Jewish Jesus*, 2019).

The Realms of Heaven

Does God open the realms of heaven through dreams and visions? If you believe the answer is yes, do you believe He still can?

God came to King Solomon through dreams. He came to Joseph through dreams. He came to John through symbolic visions. He came to Isaiah through dreams and visions, and He came to Rabbi Schneider through dreams.

God seems to reveal some of the most important messages of things to come or things of the past, to reveal hidden treasures of heaven and heavenly wisdom through dreams and visions. Some of the most important messages sent to man from heaven came in the form of dreams and/ or visions.

Arguably one of the most important stories in the Bible where the Holy Spirit, the angel of God, speaks to Joseph through a dream is in the story of the Blessed Virgin Mother Mary, who becomes pregnant with our Lord and Savior Jesus Christ. An angel visited Joseph, the husband of Mary, in a dream and told him not to be afraid to take Mary as his wife because the child in her womb was conceived of the Holy Spirit (supernaturally) (Matthew 1:20).

Imagine if Joseph had dismissed the dream as not real or as a coincidence. There's a good chance that I wouldn't be sitting here, writing this book today, nor would you be reading it because the world would have been completely destroyed by evil.

Fun Fact

Dreams continue to be a conundrum for scientists and remain unexplainable. They speculate but cannot prove or disprove the origin or essence of dreams with science, just as they still cannot explain God or black holes. Interesting correlation: God, dreams, and black holes remain a mystery to man.

> And it shall come to pass in the last days, saith God, I will pour out of my Spirit upon all flesh: and your sons and daughters shall prophesy, and your young men shall see visions and your old men shall dream dreams.

Acts 2:17

God is still God, and He will never change. He is still allowing miracles to happen in the lives of sinners and the saved. I hope you will discover this either through my life as outlined in this book or through your own.

But first, you must learn to…

Listen to the Whispers of the Holy Spirit

Sometimes the truth is hidden right before your eyes, in plain sight, but I learned that if you blink, you could miss it.

Stop your natural brain; *look* for signs (big and small).

This book was originally titled *"Flowers from Heaven."* It was the name I had chosen for the book. However, in what sort of felt like a fluke, the true name of the book magically came to me through the whispers of the Holy Spirit; so, *God's Answer to Abortion* was born.

Monday, July 24, 2013

While in my restroom, I thought I saw a white glare pass by me. And approximately one hour later, I thought I saw the same white shadow walking in the trees outside.

It was a quick shadow.

When you start to look and listen for the signs of their (the angels') spiritual presence, more signs will come to you.

A Letter from Einstein to his Friend and the World

Now he has departed from this strange world a little ahead of me. That means nothing. People like us who believe in physics know that the distinction between past, present, and future is only a stubbornly persistent illusion. Albert Einstein, letter to the family of Michele Besso, 1953

CHAPTER I

THE DEATH

November 23, 2011

I sat at my desk, horrified, wondering what happened to the beautiful baby boy I had met the night before. How could such a beautiful child die so unexpectedly? Why? I was absolutely breathless. I had never experienced an incident of this magnitude. Being from Oakland, I was no stranger to young people dying unexpectedly, but a baby, no, I had never experienced that before. I sat for several minutes, reflecting on the night before, and suddenly it hit me like a brick in my face: I was too good for him; I was too good to hold him. I was not interested in participating in any motherly-type activities. So, I never got to hold him. The closest I came to him was a mere touch of his tiny feet. I could see it vividly: I walked over to cousin K. while she was holding him, looked at him, and touched his tiny feet.

I began to cry, and the tears just started rolling down my eyes. I cried for the baby and his mother. This was so sad. How could this have happened? My cousins saddened me. All of them. How could they be so irresponsible, drinking and partying around a brand-new baby? As I sat sobbing and thinking about how this could happen to such a beautiful baby, my mind raced through every moment of the night before. I wondered, *Did cousin K. have anything to drink, and if she did, how could she be so irresponsible?* I wasn't sure if she had been drinking as well. I sincerely hoped not. My best bet was that she had a least one drink. I needed to know what happened and how this horrible nightmare could have taken place. I picked up the phone and called my cousin N., who was there that night as well.

She answered with a cracked voice that sounded as if she had been crying. "Hello, cousin," I said, "What happened last night?" She began telling the story, and as I suspected, they had been all drinking. She indicated that cousin K. really hadn't drunk much. She said she had spoken to cousin K., and cousin K. told her that she had fallen asleep on the couch with the baby lying next to her, and when she awoke the next morning, she could not wake him and that his face was blue. Fearing the worse, she called the paramedics and rushed him to the hospital. The police also arrived at the scene while she was at the hospital. They questioned cousin K. before arresting her and taking her to jail. She was later bailed out and exonerated of all charges. The death was ruled a crib death. I know my cousin would not intentionally harm her child, but her behavior that night might have been part of the problem.

Hum, speaking of problem behavior, I began reflecting on my own. Looking at my behavior that night made me cry as well. I was too good for him. I didn't want to hold him and barely touched his little foot. Who was I to think I was too cute or too good just to grab him in my arms and hold him tight while telling him that I loved him? And now, I would never get that chance again. Never. This feeling of true emptiness left a big gaping hole in my heart. Needless to say, that morning, day, and night were hard. The guilt I felt was overwhelming. The guilt of not being able to rescue him, the guilt of not holding him and comforting him, the guilt of not knowing I would never get that chance again.

The evening came, and finally, I worked up the courage to call my cousin K. Her voice was very faint and frail when she answered. But she sounded remarkably upbeat, considering the circumstances. She began explaining what happened as though it was rehearsed. She didn't go into full detail but indicated she fell asleep next to him and awoke with him looking blue all over. I could only imagine the horror a mother, who had just given birth a few weeks prior, would feel while looking at her newborn son appearing lifeless. She said she frantically called 911, who came right away and rushed the two of them to the hospital, only to discover that he was DOA, dead on arrival.

I could hear the cracking sound in her voice as she uttered the word "dead," and my face nearly broke into a million pieces. I just couldn't understand how or why this happened to such a beautiful baby. But one thing I knew for sure was that I would never be the girl I was that night again, ever. If ever I was given the opportunity to be around a beautiful baby again, I was going to be a humble person and not a conceited, arrogant, snobby human being. Moreover, I didn't know it at the time, but the death of this innocent baby would literally change my life forever.

I made sure to keep in touch with cousin K. so that I could attend the funeral. I mean, it was the least I could do under the circumstances. I didn't get to appreciate him in life, so now, maybe, I could appreciate him in death. The day of the funeral was very sad. The little chapel was beautiful and filled with the aroma of fresh flowers. The service began with the priest speaking and sharing nice words. Then there was a video display of the baby, which literally brought tears to all the eyes in the room. It seemed so unfair that his little life was snuffed away so prematurely. And the casket, so small and blue. It literally sent shock waves through my body. I had never seen anything like it before or will since. The service was brief, and the family exited the main entrance at the end.

One thing I noticed was that the parents of the child were not together; they were not friends and were not speaking at the funeral. The father actually arrived at the funeral with a new girlfriend. The parents' behavior just seemed interesting to me. The funeral ended quietly, and I left.

December 18, 2021

On this day, December 18, 2021, I finally gathered the courage to speak to my cousin to reflect on what happened the fateful night her infant son died. She provided two new insights that I had never ever known before, even while writing this book, that is, until this day.

1. The name of her son was Ethan Christopher (Christopher was his middle name). The irony of his name is crazy, as you will see later in this book.

2. The date he died was November 23, 2011. Sometime after his death, I simply forgot it, and when reflecting on the incident, I could not remember the date it actually happened.

And Then It All Began

The angelic visitations, the messengers, the dreams, the visions, the four children's stories, and the fifth child, the numbers, the symbols, the songs, the television shows, the real-life heavenly artifacts, the balloons, and the mysteries.

The dreams started sometime in 2012 and ended sometime in 2013.

In my case, I experienced both dreams and visions. I also experienced supernatural occurrences, sightings, and the findings of supernatural heavenly physical artifacts and objects that are so miraculous you probably won't believe me. But believe this: I could not make any of this up. I'm simply not that smart. I am about as normal as they come and as ordinary and extraordinary, all packaged into one.

The answers came to me through several dreams (approximately seven or eight) of one child, the same child reappearing to me in multiple recurring dreams. In all my life, this had never ever happened before, nor has it happened since. However, God did not only send revelations of the story of one child who is in heaven, but He also sent the stories of four other children who are also in heaven. Only two of the five (total children's stories) came by way of a dream. The stories of the other three came through a series of real-life earthly messengers, modern technology (television), objects, pictures, and supernatural signs. However, one of the five children's stories was partially revealed to me here on the earth and partially through a dream of heaven. I know this sounds confusing, but you will come to understand later.

I was a notorious party girl, swinger, and everything else that is atrocious today in my eyes. We were living a life on the edge to nowhere.

Party after party, girl after girl, guy after guy, night after night, day after day, month after month, and year after year. Nonstop sex, lust, drugs, fornication, parties, vanity, vainglory, selfish ambitions, and gross materialism. I know this all sounds fun now, but I assure you it is the emptiest

life one can ever live because when it is all over, you realize it was nothing more than a lie. Yes, it seemed real, fun,
and true at the moment. But when the party was over and
the sun rose the next morning, he was gone (usually to the
next female); they were gone, and I was alone. That is until
the dad came, and although he wasn't gone the next morning, he was still empty; I was still empty, and somehow it
all felt dirty, like, what did we do, and why? And how did
we make it out of that one alive and unscathed? One word,
one name, one man...Jesus.

At the time, this life felt right; it felt like fun; it felt
real. It felt so real I/we couldn't let go. It became our drug
and our intoxication. Oh, and did I mention strip clubs,
where everything that happens there stays there? Women,
be warned: it is easier for you to walk away from this lifestyle than it is for the man. You may want to walk away,
and he may not, and if you don't fulfill his need, the next
woman will.

It is said that the prayers of the saints and martyrs are a
beautiful aroma to God (Yahweh). I believe that the prayers
and voices of innocent aborted children are too.

You know the old adage: "You only live once."

Wrong

^.

We will live forever, in one place or the other. The Bible suggests that the soul never dies. The soul is God's
Word spoken into life. In the Bible, it says that in the be-

ginning, God spoke and said, "Let there be light," and there was light. He also said, "Let us make man in our image, after our likeness." And man was conceived (Genesis 1:3, 26–28). God's Word is life, and all life is the living soul, not flesh, the soul. Flesh dies; the soul doesn't. Take heed.

The First Supernatural Sign: the Angel in the Mirror

A Supernatural Angelic Visitation

This supernatural vision came before the first two messengers and all the dreams while I was still living "the life."

It was a typical morning, nothing out of the ordinary. I'm not sure what day of the week it was, but I was up pretty early, somewhere around six a.m. As I was preparing for work, I took a quick shower. After stepping out of the shower and grabbing my towel, I looked up and noticed the room was very steamy, unusually steamy, for some reason. And suddenly, I looked up at the mirror, and the most miraculous image appeared before my eyes across the entire mirror. I immediately became frozen. I stood as still as a pole, eyes fixed on the mirror, gazing at the most amazing, miraculous, angelic-looking image covering my entire bathroom mirror. I was in complete awe as I stood there for several minutes, gazing at something that I couldn't believe was really there. It was a figure completely made of steam on a glass mirror—the most beautiful angelic-looking butterfly nestled inside a large heart encrusted with diamonds. The heart was humongous and spread across the entire 180-degree mirror, which covered two large walls in the bathroom. There appeared to be an angel inside of the heart. The butterfly was larger than the angel and nestled behind the angel. It is really difficult to describe or capture the majestic beauty of a figure made completely of steam, like a Picasso or a van Gogh art piece. The angel really appeared to look like a woman—in hindsight, I can add the woman appeared to look somewhat like the Virgin Mary—a woman with her head covered by a veil, looking downward and possibly holding something in her arms. So, it was like a 3D image of a large heart, encrusted and imbued with details, the kind of details you would find in a Roman cathedral. There was a large butterfly inside the heart and an angel or an angelic figure that appeared to be a woman inside the butterfly.

The entire image was made of the steam on the mirror. The image remained on the mirror for several minutes. I was frozen as I gazed at it and wondered what it meant and why I was seeing it. I simply didn't understand what it was, why it was there, or why I was able to see it. But I couldn't take my eyes off it. I couldn't look away. It was like looking at an angel or some angelic form. Honestly, it was like a two-way double-sided butterfly made of jewels, where half of the body was on the outside of the mirror, and half of the body was on the inside of the mirror. If

I were to try to make an earthly comparison, the closest thing with such immaculate detail I can think of is one of Queen Elizabeth's jewel-studded crowns, but it was far more beautiful. I wish you were there to see it, too; the beauty and mystery of it are truly beyond words.

August 25, 2012. The Hungry Baby

When I awoke, I spoke these words out loud while letting out a deep exhale, "I just had the darndest dream."

A hungry little baby drank water and ate a whole banana. The baby ate so fast that he appeared to be starving.

I awoke.

The First Messenger

Joyce Meyer

∧

:

<>

(*)

2012

The story of a brokenhearted family in China. While sitting on my bed, channel surfing, I came upon Joyce Meyer's show, one of my favorite religious shows. Only this time, she wasn't standing behind the pulpit, preaching to an exuberant audience. She was sitting on a small stage, speaking with two other women. One sat telling a story as Joyce Meyer listened. One interesting feature that I noted (while reflecting on everything) was that Joyce Meyer was wearing a red shirt. At the moment, that detail was completely meaningless, but if my recollection of the color of her shirt is correct, that detail would later become a very significant one. Joyce was the first to be sent by God.

Ironic biblical connection: when Jesus (Yeshua) rose three days after He gave His life, the first person He appeared to was Mary Magdalene, a woman who became the messenger to the other disciples that Jesus was alive. A woman (Joyce Meyer) was the first messenger sent to me by God regarding the revelation of my assignment that was imminent.

The Second Messenger

Rabbi Schneider
<*>

2012

One Sunday morning, while flipping through television channels, I came upon a gospel channel with a Jewish rabbi speaking to me or, should I say, the television audience. What caught my eye were the candles he had lit around the podium where he stood. I thought to myself, *How comfortable and soothing.* And for this reason, before hearing him speak or knowing the content of his message, I did not change the channel. And until this day, I don't know how I ended up on a channel with Rabbi Schneider, but I now understand that he was sent to me as a messenger from God.

As I continued to listen, I found the content of his message interesting and compelling. However, my thoughts did not extend that. I just found him to be intelligent and soothing. He appeared to speak an unshakable truth. I watched and continued watching week after week. The whole series was about prophecies, dreams, and visions. Rabbi Schneider quoted a section of the Bible that said old men would dream dreams, and young men would have visions (Acts 2:17). He spoke of the last days and what would be happening to human beings. I watched until the series ended.

And then what came suddenly, and without warning or premonition, was the following: dreams; visions; supernatural signs, wonders, occurrences, mysterious artifacts, visitations, the physical state of paralysis, and messages from God.

The dreams started after the angel's visitation and the first two messengers. But before I continue with the dreams, I will take you back to where it all began. The life.

The Third Messenger

Joseph Prince, the Pastor of Grace
(*)

One day, while sitting in a hotel room (Ritz-Carlton), feeling all worthless and terrible after a night of partying, I flipped on the television, and to my surprise, there was a man preaching the gospel. I had no idea gospel shows came on regular television, on Sunday morning, in hotel rooms. However, I listened, and I promise you, his message, "I am the righteousness of God in Christ, and I can do all things through Christ who strengthens me" (Philippians 4:13, paraphrased), changed my life. I knew God had sent this message to me on this day when I needed it the most. Interestingly, as I sat listening to Pastor Joseph Prince, I recalled that I had previously had a dream where I was traveling on a long, meandering, mountainous road with Mr. N., my boyfriend. We were driving fast, and the ride was extremely bumpy and uncomfortable. I kept feeling like we were going to fall off the cliff and crash to our deaths when, suddenly, we ended up traveling in the opposite direction on a completely different highway. We were now on a broad, wide-open freeway with very few cars traveling on it. As we drove, I suddenly saw a beautiful white hotel off in the distance. I looked at Mr. N. and said, "We should go there because it looks so tropical and beautiful with large green leafy trees completely surrounding it." I really wanted to make reservations to go there.

Real Life, Not a Dream

I can't make this up. One evening, when Mr. N. and I were returning from a road trip, we passed a tiny church with a huge, brightly illuminated green-and-white sign that read, "Grace." The sign was the same color as the hotel I had seen in my dream.

The Life That Started It All

The Swingers

-

Mr. N. and I were living life on the edge. We had become swingers, yes, bona fide swingers, living the full swinger lifestyle: sex, strip clubs, wild parties. I guess you could say my life went on without skipping a beat after the faint pain in my body left, and I felt normal again. The memory of the abortion was gone. So far gone, it was as though it never even happened.

This section has deliberately been shortened because I, in no way, want to glamorize the swinger or maverick lifestyle. But because of its relevance, I think it is only fair that I provide a vivid picture of just how awful and callous our hearts and lives were. On a typical party night, we would dress to the nines and head to Sunset Boulevard or another venue's location. On a night like this, Mr. N.

was extremely focused on completing our mission, which was to get a woman or willing participant to engage in our scandalous undertaking. Honestly, we didn't have to work hard at all; usually, it was fairly easy to find a willing participant.

Mr. N. made his classic move by finding a female of interest to dance with him. He began dancing with a female he had identified as being voluptuous and curvy. Their sexy dancing usually went on for several minutes before I joined them on the dance floor. The three of us danced and drank all night. While in the moment, we found this sinful behavior as great and fun; we felt untouchable, invincible, and as if there was nothing that could come between our lustful pursuits and physical happiness. The night went on with music, dance, and alcohol. At the end of clubbing and parties, we typically continued the wicked escapades into the nights. This behavior went on for many days, months, and years. At the time, Mr. N. and I thought we were a hot couple just doing what was natural to adults. But deep down inside my heart, I knew that what we were doing was wrong. Somehow, I always maintained a sense of Christ's identity. This means that because of my Christian mother, I had accepted Christ in my heart from birth.

Hindsight is definitely twenty-twenty vision; that said, there were no winners in any of those situations, on any of those nights, in any of those houses. And had our souls been required of us on any one of those given nights, or had God allowed Satan to have his way with us (sift us like wheat until our flesh was destroyed), I assure you we would have died and gone to hell that night.

Oops

)-:

"Shush, shush, shush," I calmly whispered to myself. "What have I done"?

Thinking, *Why did I tell him that? Now look at what I've done*, I grabbed my head on both sides and slumped over on my knees in utter despair. *What an inconvenience, what a darn inconvenience. How could I let this happen? Oh well*, I thought, *no worries, this problem is very easy to solve.* And without any hesitation, I began making plans to solve this life-altering problem. Yes, as you probably have guessed already, I was pregnant. I sat thinking, *How did this happen? What went wrong?* I didn't think I was that fertile and it would happen to me. Boy, was I a fool! I had been having unprotected sex for a number of years after my first two children and had not gotten pregnant. So how could this happen now? And why now?

Planned Parenthood to the rescue. "Yoo-hoo!" I shouted. I had it all figured out. I would call and make an appointment for an abortion first thing in the morning. I'll make sure they schedule me for the abortion at the first opportunity that the abortion could be done safely. Typically, at six weeks of gestation. How ironic that I was thinking of safety but the safety of who? Definitely not the child in my womb.

The Rationalization

O
^_^

There's no real life in me yet because it's still just a tiny little seed or cell that is not yet a life or living flesh.

The Thinking Continues...

After several minutes of thinking about what I intended to do, I wondered about the life inside my body and began to question myself if it was even really a life yet. Thinking out loud, I said, "I mean, it isn't really a life yet (right?) since it's still just a tiny seed or cluster of cells. Like a seed of a plant, it isn't really a plant or a tree until the seed grows into a plant or a tree (right?). If I remove the seed from the soil before it grows into a plant, then where is the harm in that? After all, it wasn't a plant yet, right?

"I will remove the seed before it grows into a plant; thus, all I have to do is simply remove the seed and not an actual life. It will just be a speck or a seed; there will be no pain for it or me. Thus, all will be well, and I will continue to live my life as usual and with no hiccups. Secondly, I will actually be saving the life of the child because who wants to be born into a world with unwilling parents? Or, better stated, parents who really don't want this child. I have no money to take care of another child, and this is simply too soon to get pregnant by a man I really had just met a few months ago.

"I am not going to do it. That's it: I just can't."

The plan was set. I called the clinic and easily made the appointment. I scheduled the appointment on the last day of the sixth week of my unwanted pregnancy. On the day of the abortion, my boyfriend very happily accompanied me to the abortion clinic because he didn't want this headache any more than I did.

Food for Thought

%\?+

If my thinking was correct and what I was carrying inside my womb was simply a seed and not quite a human being as yet, why was I experiencing the same feeling in my body that I experienced with my living son, the son that I did not abort? The feeling that is caused by the body preparing the female for the baby, who will need feeding and nurturing while inside the mother's womb. This is the problem with "rationalization." It allows human beings to make sense of absolute nonsense. It allows us to believe our own lies and make what is true a lie and what is a lie the truth and still be able to live with ourselves mentally without shame, guilt, remorse, or accountability. And this is the sad truth. Hence think about slavery and the Holocaust.

The Drive to the Clinic

++===
*--o

The drive to the abortion clinic was a bit nerve-wracking. I was nervous and simply wanted to get it over with. I couldn't wait until the part where I woke up from this nightmare, and the problem or, should I say, the bad dream ended. Unfortunately, the bad dream I was referring to was inside my stomach. I was so heartless and stoic I didn't even think of that who was in my stomach as a child at all; I simply referred to it as "it." Because I did not recognize the life inside of me as a life, I never used the word "life" when referring to the living soul inside my womb because the child inside of me simply didn't matter to me at all. All that mattered to me was that I continued living my life as I saw fit.

Mr. N., well, he had nothing to say, nothing at all. I believe he was a little shell-shocked; thus, we drove in silence: not one word was spoken between us. I think he was thinking the same thing I was: *I just want to hurry up and get this over with. I don't want any more children, baby–momma drama, or the financial responsibilities of having a child.*

We barely knew each other; I mean, a few months here or there, either way, it was not enough time to have a child together. It simply was not the right time for either of us.

I remember what he was wearing: a red hoodie sweatshirt with a white T-shirt, blue jeans, and white Nikes.

The drive was short because the clinic was located just a few miles away from my home in West Los Angeles. In addition to feeling nervous, I was feeling really, really sick. I guess it was morning sickness. Yes, at six weeks of gestation, I was feeling morning sickness, which is caused by increased hormones in the female's body during the first trimester of pregnancy (first six weeks).

CHAPTER 2

THE CLINIC

;-;

The abortion clinic was designed to be very comfortable and cozy for the patient. The room was lit well with warm lighting. The couches and chairs were soft, cushy, and comfortable. There was a beautiful, vibrant, luminous salt-water aquarium filled with brightly colored fish and a colorful coral reef. It was alive with beauty and life. How ironic that a place of absolute horror and death for so many children contained life in the form of a coral reef (which, to the naked eye, doesn't seem alive at all, but it is absolutely alive and breathing). I particularly focused on the bright-yellow fish. For some reason, they created an extra sense of comfort and ease for me. If the intention of the clinic's designer was to create a comfortable environment to help relieve the female patients of their distress and ease their minds of any discomfort, he or she succeeded.

The surgical room was cold, cold, cold. It was the complete opposite of the lounge area. It was very brightly lit and filled with surgical equipment, expensive-looking surgical equipment. I literally had to wear socks and get a warm blanket to help keep me warm. My comfort was extremely important to the clinic staff and me. I was asked to remove all my clothing and put on the special medical gown that had been provided to me by the nursing staff. The doctor and two medical staff came into the room and guided me to the surgical table. My legs and feet were then lifted onto special foot holders. Of course, this is the part where I became extremely nervous and anxious. I couldn't stop looking around the room and couldn't stop the physical shivering. It was all scary and unreal; I couldn't believe I was lying there. Somehow it felt like I was about to be suctioned out of my own womb. I tried to stop the anxiety and heavy breathing before I caused myself to have a meltdown.

"Hello, Taylor, I am Doctor Luther [name purposely changed], and I am going to perform your abortion today. How are you feeling?"

I replied, "Okay."

"Great," he replied. The doctor explained that I was about to be put to sleep using general anesthesia: "Now, the next thing that is going to happen is the anesthesiologist will be providing you with the medicine for general anesthesia so that you won't feel a thing. The procedure will take less than an hour, and afterward, you will need to go home and rest."

I replied, "Okay," feeling somewhat comforted by

his words, "no pain" and "afterward, rest." That was all I wanted: for this nightmare to be over.

The nurse walked over to me and prepared me for the anesthesia, which was inserted by a needle into my vein. The last I remember was the doctor putting on gloves, standing next to a machine, and the surgical table filled with shiny silver objects, which appeared very sharp. I thought to myself, *Thank God, I will be asleep and not be allowed to feel any pain.*

Approximately one to two hours later, I awoke in a small room, still covered with a small blanket. There was a tray sitting next to my bed, which contained graham crackers and apple juice. A clinic-staff worker entered my room and began calling my name, "La Trina, can you hear me? You are all done; the procedure was successful, and within thirty minutes, you will be ready to go home." I was still very groggy from the anesthesia, so I simply whispered out a soft "okay." I remember eating the crackers, which were very soothing. I couldn't wait to get home to my warm cozy bed. It was over.

Today, as I sit here, writing this book, I now know that it was not okay what we (parents) did.

For Mr. N. and me, the feeling was a great relief, but for that unborn baby who lay inside me—I didn't know it then, but I know it now—it was as if being crushed by a red diesel truck, broken into bits and pieces, and thrown away.

And that night, we went home, ate and drank, and slept without our hearts ever skipping a beat. Within the next day or so, I returned to my life as usual. In hindsight, while writing this book and thinking back: maybe it is Mr. N. and me (not the child in my womb) who should have suffered the agony and pain of being irresponsible parents and bearing all the burden we deserved for living outside of God's will and having unwed or unprotected sex.

More Food for Thought

%O\-

Question: *Who is more guilty, the executioner or the one who orders the execution?*

Jesus said one doesn't have to commit the sin physically for it to be sin. He said even if one thinks of the sin with their minds and hearts, that, too, is the same as actually committing the sin itself: "But I say unto you, that whosoever looketh on a woman to lust after her hath committed adultery with her already in his heart" (Matthew 5:28).

This means that our sins start in our minds and hearts. Thus, if you support sin and crime with your heart and mind, it is the same as committing the sin with your hands and body in God's eyes.

Seven Years Later

—*

It all started happening. Unbeknownst to myself, my assignment was imminent. God had given me the assignment.

It all began with the messengers, people whom I believe God, Yeshua, and the Holy Spirit sent to me to reveal the secrets of heaven that would soon be unlocked and opened to me, secret revelations of God's thoughts and feelings regarding aborted children who reside in heaven. I believe this was done in order that my soul and life might be saved as well as those of all human beings.

Very tearfully, after several months of pondering weird and crazy dreams, unexplained encounters while walking in social settings or the forest, strange movies, television shows of certain content, weird sightings, sad hunting songs, a shadowy figure floating through my home, and a steamy mirror filled with an image of such breathtaking immaculate beauty that I truly cannot describe it here on paper, I began to wonder if what I was encountering was God, Yeshua, and the Holy Spirit. Messages were being sent to me through several forms of communication. I truly cannot explain any of it. It is all still so mysterious, supernatural, awesome, and amazing.

But First, Can God Really Speak to Us through Dreams?

<*>

God came to Solomon and Joseph through dreams.

"In Gibeon the LORD appeared to Solomon in a dream by night: and God said, Ask what I shall give thee" (Kings 3:5).

God spoke to Joseph through four dreams to reveal to him that Mary was pregnant with Jesus, the Savior of Israel and the world, by way of the supernatural Holy Spirit.

"The angel of the Lord appeared unto him in a dream, saying, Joseph, thou son of David, fear not to take unto thee Mary thy wife: for that which is conceived in her is of the Holy Ghost" (Matthew 1:20).

The First Child's Story

∧

The first child is on the top right side of the picture on the cover.

Here is the story of the brokenhearted family in China, as depicted by my first messenger, Joyce Meyer, one afternoon on her television show.

Joyce Meyer and a guest speaker told the story of a teenage mother in China. One woman spoke of a young girl in China who had become pregnant by her boyfriend at the tender age of fourteen. According to my memory, this was the girl's age. I was not recording notes while watching and listening to the show because, honestly, I had no idea of the supernatural connection this show would later have to my life or of the importance of the message.

Becoming pregnant as a teenager or when unwed was extremely taboo in China and severely looked down upon. The girl did not want to disappoint her parents and was deeply frightened about her secret pregnancy being discovered. So, she went about life as usual as she continued school and remained pregnant. By wearing layered clothing, and possibly due to her small frame, she was successful in concealing the pregnancy from her parents. Nevertheless, she carried her baby through the full term (nine months).

Finally, on the day she was to give birth, she did give birth but not in a hospital. She gave birth to her baby girl in her bathroom toilet, where she let her drown immediately after birth. After the baby girl died, she wrapped her in a tight wrapping (possibly blankets).

Sadly, I believe the teenage girl's mother knew something was wrong; however, she had no idea her daughter was pregnant. The teenage mom returned to her life as usual, without skipping a beat or revealing to her parents what she had done. After a few months had passed, her mother, while cleaning her daughter's room and the house, noticed a weird smell in the house, but she could not figure out what it was. Day after day, the odor became stronger and stronger. The foul smell lingered through the home for approximately six months, with the teen girl's mother looking fervently to find the source of the smell. So, one day, while cleaning her daughter's room, she noticed the smell was particularly strong in her room.

So, she began looking under and over every pillow, the bed, and the girl's desk. She looked everywhere to no avail. Finally, while searching in the closet, she noticed the malodorous smell became stronger and stronger. She knew at that moment that whatever the smell was, it was definitely in the closet. Finally, she came upon a lump of blankets, which she removed from a top shelf in the closet, and began unwrapping and removing the blankets. And there, hidden inside, was the body of a little deceased baby girl. To use the word "shocked" would simply not be enough to define the mother's emotional state in that moment. She was completely flabbergasted, saddened, and frightened by the discovery.

Shortly after the teenage girl's mother found the baby's body, the girl told her parents what had happened, and the little baby's body was taken to the authorities. The teenage mom was incarcerated for murder, the murder of her own baby. I am not sure if she received a life sentence; however, I believe the woman speaking to Joyce said she did. This was truly one of the most tragic and moving stories that I had ever heard in my life. I had no idea in that moment and while listening to the story that it would later have a deeper supernatural meaning and connection to my life. I had no idea that Joyce Meyer was actually delivering a supernatural message from the Holy Spirit to me.

As you know, hindsight is twenty-twenty vision. With that said, the little baby girl's story would be the first of the four children's stories that God, Yeshua, and the Holy Spirit would send to me. Actually, the first story of five children, but the fifth child's story is a bit different from the other four. Later, all the pieces to the puzzle and God's hidden messages would slowly start to come together and make sense. The revelation of God's voice, as well as my supernatural prophetic assignment, was imminent.

Remember this name, "Sparkle Eyes." You will hear it again. Below you will see a picture of her. She is in the top right corner, wearing a red shirt.

The Color Red: The Mysterious Supernatural Connection

Joyce Meyer, when telling the story of the teenage mom and her baby in China, was wearing a red shirt. Sparkle Eyes, the little girl in the picture (who I believe is the little baby drowned in the toilet by her teenage mother), is also wearing a red shirt. The color of China's flag is red. Can I explain this irony? No. But I know for certain, without any doubt, that every single detail woven into the fabric of this story, as well as my story, and all of the supernatural experiences to follow have a significant spiritual meaning to them, a very complex meaning leading to a simple truth. The picture will be explained in more detail later.

Do Names Have Meaning?

I am sure you are wondering how I came up with the name Sparkle Eyes. I didn't. It was given to me by the Holy Spirit. While looking at her picture, I kept hearing the name Sparkle Eyes, and suddenly while looking at her picture, I noticed a little shimmer on her face. Thus, I knew the voice that kept nudging me was the voice of the Holy Spirit, speaking the name to me, providing the child's name. No, I didn't hear the voice audibly; I heard it spoken to me supernaturally by the Holy Spirit in my mind.

It is my belief that all names have meanings, sometimes hidden meanings, meanings that are unknown to us, but nevertheless, the meaning is always significant. Take, for instance, Jabez in the Bible. The name Jabez means "pain." Jabez was conceived in pain; therefore, his mother named him Jabez, which literally hunted Jabez throughout his life until he prayed the curse away by asking for God's hand to be with him and keep him from harm so that he would be free from pain (1 Chronicles 4:9–10).

Jesus's Name Is Yeshua

The most important name of all is Jesus's actual name, Yeshua, which I believe means "life":

YES = He is

H = the breath of God that is life

U = for all human beings, and

A = we are the apple of God's eye.

This is the most beautiful name ever spoken.

There are four children with Yeshua in the picture that I received in the mail from the Congregation of the Priests of the Sacred Heart. I will explain the card in more detail later. The fifth child, whose story was also revealed to me but at a later date than those of the other four children, is not in the picture. The fifth child's picture will be shown later in the book.

I believe each child's story was sent to me supernaturally by God the Father, God the Son, and God the Holy Spirit. You have just heard the first of the five children's stories that will be revealed to you in this supernatural prophetic book. Remember: God said that we must walk by faith and not by sight (2 Corinthians 5:7), so that is what I decided to do. All of it was hard for me to fathom initially.

A man who can only believe in what
he sees cannot believe even in his own breath,
which he cannot see.

CHAPTER 3

MYSTERIOUS ORDER OF THE CHILDREN'S STORIES

Best Wishes for Back to School

One point that must be made is the stories of the four children featured in the picture did not come to me in any specific order that I could make any sense of. I am sure now that there was a supernatural meaning to the order in which the Holy Spirit revealed each story to me, but I am still unsure of the hidden meaning. I will speak more about this later. Most importantly, it must be noted that each story came to me without any provocation, prior knowledge, or experience that I had had in my life before. To be honest, I had no idea that I would ever receive a card from priests. And I certainly was not aware of any of the children pictured on the card or that they even had a story that would later be told to the world, and definitely, not by me.

Remember: there is no word for "coincidence" in the Hebrew Bible.

Like the universe, everything involving God is intended and has a meaning and a purpose.

After I received the first two children's stories, I began looking at the picture quite differently. I started to wonder if the other children in the picture had a story and if or when their stories would be revealed to me. It was at this time that I really started believing that something beyond this world was happening. Something supernatural. This was when I began looking for and listening to signs of the

Holy Spirit a lot closer.

The events in this book are being written chronologically, as they actually occurred. Thus, the order of events revealed in this book may not make any logical or sequential sense at all. The times in which each event happened were completely outside of my control. Thus, the stories, dreams, documentaries, messengers, visions, mysterious happenings, signs, and wonders may oscillate. But I must document the events as they actually occurred, so please bear with me.

The First Supernatural Movie

A Documentary: Einstein (2008)

-/\-

"I want to know God's thoughts in a mathematical way"

(Albert Einstein).

$$E = Mc^2$$

One night, while watching television and flipping through the channels, I came upon a documentary about Einstein. The show was just starting, and for some reason, I felt compelled to watch it. Besides, I've always had a thing for smart people, space, stars, and the unknown. The documentary chronicled his life from birth to death. The scientists discussed one of Einstein's most famous equations, $E = Mc^2$. One scientist said that Einstein, in his studies, discovered that E (energy) becomes M (mass) and c^2, which is the speed of light squared. This means the process repeats, whereby mass can become energy and energy can become mass at the speed of light. The way I understood this (and I am no physicist) is that everything starts as energy, which becomes mass at the speed of light, and when the mass is no longer mass, it returns to being energy, also at the speed of light. Thus, this process cannot be seen by the human eye. I also read somewhere that even masses at rest have energy inherent to them.

They went on to say that this ($E = Mc^2$) is the engine that lights up the stars. One other thing that stood out to me was that Einstein is also famously known for saying that he was fascinated with the universe because he wanted to know God's thoughts.

Initially, the documentary was nothing more than entertainment for me. At the time, I wasn't trying to make any connections between the documentary or the Holy Spirit or why the Holy Spirit sent it to me in the first place. It wasn't until much later in my supernatural experience that I reflected back on everything that had previously happened during my initial journey. And the one thing I remembered, which became very salient, was that this particular documentary was the very first of all the documentaries and movies to be sent to me.

When I began writing the book (three or four years later), I pondered for hours as to why. I began to question why this documentary of all the documentaries and movies that were sent to me was the very first to be sent. But mysteriously, whenever I had a question, the Holy Spirit would answer. The only answer provided to me was as follows: this documentary contained within it a secret of God, the secret of life and the secret of death, and thereafter, the secret of how all living life (human, animals, etc.) begins and began.

"In the beginning was the Word, and the Word was with God, and the Word was God" (John 1:1).

Think...

Can words in the spoken form be seen? No, they cannot. They can only be heard. Thus, what does this mean? Words in the spoken form are pure energy. And what is energy? The breath (in word form) or unseen substances moving at the speed of light. Thus, *energy* is God. Thus, the meaning of why this documentary was the first to be revealed to me is because God, simply put, God is first. The true origin of life was being revealed to me by way of this documentary.

The Bible says, "Death and life are in the power of the tongue" (Proverbs 18:21). God's breath is life, and when He breathes life into mass (the human body or, at the initial stages of development, the human cells that lie within the mother's womb), the mass, or lump of cells, becomes life.

Thus, God was explaining to me (before revealing the rest of my story) that all life begins as energy (God's breath) and that "a lump of cells" (as some would refer to it) is actually God's breath and a human being in the very initial stage of development.

Boy, was I a fool! What was I thinking? Did I think that it was me who made the life that existed within my body, within my womb? I didn't understand the origin of life. And if all of this sounds out of touch for you, try it for yourself. Speak to someone and ask them if they can see the breath that flows out of your mouth while you are speaking. Or simply blow on your hand. Did you see anything? Probably not. Nor did I when I tried it. However, the air or breath that came from your mouth is your life and the breath of God. Without it, you would die. Ask anyone who has ever drowned.

More Food for Thought

What is the spirit? What is the soul? E = energy. Can you see either the spirit or the soul? "No" is the obvious answer. Speaking of the flesh: mass (M) is obviously something that can be seen, felt, and touched. Mass turns back to energy; thus, c^2 means that the process of mass (M) becoming (I) (E) energy for the second time is the death of the human flesh (physical death). The first time when (I) (E) energy transforms is at the initial stage of life and when the (I) human is conceived in the mother's womb. Thus, the second time (I) (E) energy transforms is when our souls leave our bodies and ascend or descend to the second heaven, where they are either in their final resting place or await their final resting place as a result of physical death. I do not profess to know whether there is a purgatory or if, as the Bible says, when a believer dies, they are with God in heaven.

Note: Always Pay Attention to the Subtle Details

Notice the deliberate and apparent issue in the above paragraph: I did not intentionally include the (I). That (I) was not typed by me. I know what you're thinking: "Okay, well, how did it get there?" Yes, that is a good question. I typed the paragraph and moved on to typing the rest of the book. When I returned to my computer sometime later, while continuing with my edits, as I scanned the pages, I came upon the above paragraph. To my astonishment, I noticed that the passage was not making any sense. So, as I looked closely, I noticed that everywhere I typed the word "energy," an (I) had mysteriously appeared before the word "energy." The (I) was not originally placed in parentheses. I decided, instead of removing the letter (I) due to it being an obvious mistake, to leave all of the (I)'s in the place where I found them and add parentheses. The reasons for this decision were due to the fact that: number one, the

(I) was placed everywhere the (E) for energy was placed; number two, how could it be a mistake I made if that same mistake happened several times in the paragraph? Number three, there is no word for "coincidence" in the Bible, and number four, I recalled that in the Bible, Jesus sometimes referred to Himself as "I AM." Thus, I perceived this eerie or unexplained mistake was no mistake and no coincidence; it was God. No, I had not conducted a find-and-replace command. Had that been the case, the entire book would have been affected by the same mistake. The only place I found this is in the above paragraph.

I realize this sounds nutty (LOL), yes, I understand, but the better you come to know God, the more sense miracles start to make. But take heed.

Remember the story of Noah in the Bible:

But as the days of Noah were, so also will the coming of the Son of Man be. For as in the days before the flood, they were eating and drinking, marrying and giving in marriage, until the day that Noah entered the ark.

Matthew 24:37–38

Hence, everyone was busy living their lives, and there are some who believe people mocked Noah as he was building the ark. Allegedly, the people mocking Noah are not in the Bible.

The Souls' Gateway

I believe the soul enters and leaves the human body (and that of animals) through the gateway of our nostrils. There are two reasons that I believe and know this for sure. The first reason is because the Bible scriptures say so. In Genesis 2:7, the Bible says, "Then the Lord God formed man of the dust of the ground and breathed into his nostrils the breath of life, and man became a living soul."

The second reason is due to a supernatural experience I had one night while driving down a long meandering road in Oakland, California, on my way to the airport to fly back home to Los Angeles, California.

Suddenly, I Was Brought to a Screeching Halt by God (Yahweh)

God sends a gentle (subtle) correction: October 29, 2021, at 3:15 p.m.

Reflect for a moment on the paragraph written earlier under the caption "More Food for Thought." That entire section that begins with the words "What is the spirit?" was written on October 29, 2021, around 3:15 p.m.

The following paragraphs (typed by me) were sent to me supernaturally by God, Yeshua, and the Holy Spirit on that same day, October 29, 2021, at approximately 7:13 p.m. when I arrived home from work:

On October 29, 2021, at 4:53 p.m., I spotted a praying mantis sitting on my left front tire.

On October 29, 2021, at 7:13 p.m., Rabbi Manis Friedman delivered God's message (correction) to me.

Read carefully: October 29, 2021; 7:13 p.m.

So, after arriving home, I went about my business as usual. To help pass the time, I was going to talk to Mr. N., but he was unwilling. So, I called my dad, but when I did, his background noise was so intolerable—as he prepared his evening dinner—I was forced to hang up on him within a few minutes. Thus, I was forced to prepare for my evening activities in silence. "Ah-ha," I said, thinking out loud, "I will go to YouTube and watch some of my friend's videos, so a least I'll have some background noise to keep me company." So, I picked up my phone and started browsing through the YouTube channels to see if I could find my friend's page. However, while looking for her page, I happened to stumble upon a Jewish man with a video titled "Where Do Souls Come From." And of course, I was immediately intrigued by the title because I had just finished the chapter in this book about the human soul and its origins. *How ironic,* I thought, *that I have come across a title like this, being that I am just writing about the same content.* So, instead of continuing to my friend's page, I stopped to listen to the rabbi. His name was Rabbi Manis Friedman. And when his video, dated October 26, 2021, started playing, I almost fainted. I could not believe *what*

I was hearing.

God's Correction and Another Supernatural Confirmation That the Angels Are Always Listening

I literally could not believe what I was hearing. The very first question the rabbi posed to the audience was, "What happens at the end of life?" Hence, is there life after death? Rabbi Friedman suggested that the question in and of itself was flawed. He indicated the question in and of itself is misworded. Because, as he indicated, life doesn't die. He went on to say, "If you're asking if there is life after death, the answer is no because what is dead is dead, and what is alive s alive."

My rendition: life is God; all life is God, and God is eternal; therefore, life is eternal. Okay, yes, I know that sounds like what I said on the preceding pages. But here's the kicker:

The rabbi posed the following questions:

"What is life?" Life is, purely, soul.

"Where does life *go*?" "What happens when life leaves?"

"What dies and what lives?"

But with all the questions being asked, I became even more alert when he posed the following question: "What happens when life *comes*?"

I am deliberately paraphrasing here. He suggested that

in order to appreciate what happens when life leaves, we must first understand what happens when life comes. He went on to say that in order to understand one, we must understand the other. He indicated (based on the Hebrew Torah) that when God created the first human being, He created the body out of the earth and then breathed into it a living soul. The rabbi indicated that the human body is not a living thing but, rather, clay (a hundred pounds or so).

Chronological Order of God's Message (Correction) Sent to Me through a Messenger, the Jewish Rabbi

1. Life comes from God; He breathes life into the clay (human body) that becomes a living soul. *Hence, God didn't speak life into humans; He breathed life into humans.* He didn't say, "Let it come alive; let it live." Of all other creation, He said, "Let there be…" and it was.

2. The common between speaking and breathing is that both involve breath. *But the breath we use for speech is the surface breath (superficial breath). The rabbi used balloons as an example of the deeper breath (the inner breath).* You will see later in this book that prior to ever seeing the rabbi's video, I was fascinated with balloons and how they became a part of my supernatural wonders and experience. **I nearly fainted when the rabbi included**

the following: "In scientific terms, Einstein came up with this brilliant insight where he says the universe is made up of mass and energy, different kinds of mass and different kinds of energy." So, he went on to explain what I previously said about energy becoming mass and vice versa ($E = Mc^2$).

3. He continued by saying that mass dissolving into energy does not include life and that life is not energy. *Life is a completely different entity, different from mass, different from energy. Life is a living entity that, in the human being, is composed of ten or more functions, hence a soul.* What is a soul? A living being who thinks, feels, and behaves. Hence, the soul is life that comes into the body. How and when does the soul come into the body? Conception? When does life begin?

4. *According to the Jewish rabbi, life begins forty days before conception: the soul is told that it is going to be born.* It has time to acclimate to the idea that it is leaving heaven and that it is going to be born into the physical world. The soul doesn't like this and is not thrilled by the idea, but it does have time to get used to it.

5. *So, when does the birth of a child begin?* Essentially, forty days before conception. The rabbi noted that the Torah indicates that every time a woman was given a blessing that she was going to have a

child, she was always told, "This time next year," which equaled twelve months. The gestation period doesn't take twelve months. The part of the gestation period that we know about takes nine months or less in some cases. But regarding the living soul, it takes more than nine months to allow the soul time to get adjusted before it goes from heaven to heaven—before it leaves the third heaven (godly realm) and arrives at the earthly heaven, the first realm.

"At the moment of conception, the soul is complete. Life is life; there is no partial life. The soul is never underdeveloped; the soul is always complete" (Rabbi Manis Friedman, "The Soul and Its Life," YouTube, 2021).

The rabbi said that at the moment of conception, the soul is completely matured and the body hardly exists. Thus, this means that when a woman has a baby, the first thing we do is completely spiritual and hardly physical at all. He added that for this reason, the scientific explanation of conception is very much inadequate because it only describes the body, the natural, not the supernatural.

He noted the Bible scripture where King David indicated that his mother and father abandoned him, but God gathered him in: "When my father and my mother forsake me, then the LORD will take me up" (Psalm 27:10). The rabbi went on to say that the above statement means that David remembered the moment and experience of being conceived.

Wow, isn't it amazing that the rabbi's words in this passage go hand in hand with the subject matter of my book, which I started writing (in note form only) sometime in 2012, and the above passage was given to me by the rabbi in 2021? Interesting, to say the least.

The little human being at conception is experiencing the most dramatic and traumatic moment of its existence. It has made contact with the physical world. The rabbi continued that although King David's parents were asleep and abandoned him, God was in the womb, guiding him and his experience, and that reassured him, and he was able to continue to develop in the womb.

1. "From the moment of conception, the embryo (I realize 'embryo' is not the scientific term for this stage of development, but I refuse to use the scientific name here, which sounds more like an alien) hears everything, sees everything, feels everything, and understands everything" because it is a complete soul (Friedman, "The Soul and Its Life"). The rabbi went on to say that all of those activities are soul activities.

The Soul

"The eye doesn't see; the soul sees through the eye.
The soul thinks in the brain, and it feels in the heart"
(Friedman, "The Soul and Its Life").

He then said that the soul hears through the ear and speaks through the mouth. It is the soul doing all of the above, not the body parts. The rabbi suggested the embryo hears the conversations that its parents are having better because it is not listening with the ears since the ears haven't developed yet. Thus, when the child is born, it will hear through the ear, but not as well as it did while it heard with the soul.

Where does the soul get its energy from? The rabbi's answer is from energy. Where does it get its life from? Life.

Order of events as they occurred on October 29, 2021:

3:15 p.m. I wrote the section of this book titled
"Think…" that describes the origin of life and
the soul's gateway into the human body.

4:53 p.m. While entering my vehicle, I came upon a
praying mantis sitting on my left front tire. Of
course, I saved it by moving it to a safe place
before taking off. However, at the moment,
I didn't realize it was a praying mantis until

I Googled it. See my Instagram video (@ godsanswertoabortion). The video was made simply because I thought it looked cool, but not because, at the moment, I knew it would have any supernatural significance.

7:13 p.m. I incidentally (supernaturally) turned to a YouTube channel with a video titled "Life is Purely the Soul" by Rabbi Manis Friedman.

11:06 p.m. I looked up the insect that I had saved and discovered it was a praying mantis.

The Three Additional Revelations of God's Supernatural Correction Sent to Me

What happened next is really not easy to explain. However, two of God's revelations were revealed to me at the end of this supernatural and miraculous experience.

The Angels and the Holy Spirit Are Always Watching

The angels and the Holy Spirit are always listening and watching our every move. I had literally just finished writing the six paragraphs about the soul, and then the miracle began right after. This means the Holy Spirit was there with me as I wrote; otherwise, how could the correction happen so fast?

The Mystery of Speaking in Tongues Revealed

Have you ever been so grateful for something that you couldn't stop thanking the person who gave you the special gift? That is how I felt when the video stopped playing. I immediately began walking around my room, more like dancing, thanking God. I began with an English thank-you (one only), and suddenly, I became so overwhelmed with a feeling of joy and amazement that I literally felt as if I had slipped into a trance. I couldn't speak in human form. I began speaking in utterances, or should I say, singing, and I couldn't stop myself. I continued singing in an unknown language that sounded akin to a Native American chant during their spiritual dances. This went on for approximately fifteen or twenty minutes. I had never really spoken in tongues and had never really been a person who thought I could speak in tongues. I never wanted to seem phony or fake, so I usually just avoided it. But what I always knew was that when it was my time to speak in tongues, God would reveal the secret of tongues to me. And this is what He did on this day, in that moment. I now understand that speaking in tongues means the soul gains control over physical flesh (mind and body). Once your soul is in control, it begins to speak to God, Yeshua, the Holy Spirit, and the angels.

The language will not be known by man until he is in heaven. It is my belief that English is not the language of heaven.

God's Revelation to the Rabbi, Orthodox Jews, and Nonbelieving Jews

To be very honest with you: I really struggled with writing this revelation. Number one, I didn't want to come off as offensive to anyone. And number two, I simply don't feel important enough to be the one giving a message to one of the most intelligent people groups on the face of the earth, Yahweh's chosen people, the Orthodox Jews, all Jewish people. But I was not able to escape it; in other words, the thought came without warning or my will, hence nothing that I would think in the natural. Thus, I knew it was from God and knew the story of the miraculous supernatural moment with the praying mantis would not be complete without this final piece. So here it is.

Miraculous beyond Belief Message from God (Yahweh) to Nonbelieving Jews

Do you notice anything crazily ironic? Look carefully: the rabbi's name is *Manis*, and the insect I saved exactly seven hours before was a praying *mantis*. The even crazier part is the only difference in the names is the letter *t*. The letter (*t* or *T*) looks like the one symbol, shape, Yeshua is always associated with—the cross (T). And if you want to hear something even crazier that goes along with all of the above: Rabbi Manis is an Orthodox Jew who has not accepted Jesus, Yeshua, as the Messiah as of yet. He still holds that the Messiah has yet to come. Whether it is irony or a hidden message, the only letter separating the names is the (T) symbol of the cross. And which of the two has that particular letter missing from their name, the praying mantis or Rabbi Manis?

See how mysterious God is. Everything in the universe (even insects) worship Yahweh and Yeshua and accept Yeshua as the risen Messiah. How do I know this? Who ordered the praying mantis to sit on my car tire? How long was it sitting there? Who knows. The point is it had been given an assignment; I was its assignment; it had a message to deliver to me from God. Prior to this day, I have never encountered a praying mantis.

God's message to the Orthodox Jew is he/she is not yet complete. They are missing one thing: the *T*, hence the cross and the acceptance of Yeshua as their Lord and Savior, who came, died on the cross, was risen from the dead by the Holy Spirit, ascended to heaven, and sits at the right hand of the throne of Yahweh. In order for the Orthodox Jews to be complete as God's chosen people, they must come to this realization before the end.

This was very hard to write, but it was placed before

my eyes as part of my assignment; thus, when God speaks, we must listen.

This is how the mystery of God works—at least, what I can gather and understand from it all. Secrets are miraculously revealed in the blink of an eye, in a moment, in a day, through multiple moving pieces (like a puzzle) that had to be solved. In the Bible, Yeshua often used parables to reveal hidden messages to provoke the listener into deeper thought and understanding.

A Prophetic and Tragic Supernatural Experience

:...(

I have included this supernatural experience because it falls in line with what I have been discussing about life and the living soul. The experience was so jolting I truly believe it was God sending me a message of things to come in my life in the future. In hindsight, I can see that God has been with me every step of my life, talking to me through the Holy Spirit and supernatural signs. It feels like He was providing subtle answers to questions that I had either already asked or would one day ask. This experience was a foresight of more supernatural awakenings to come in the future.

A Throwback Experience That Set the Foundation for My Future Assignment

Do Animals Go to Heaven, and Do They Souls?

I exited the Interstate 580 freeway at the top of the mountain and began driving downward. I was driving a rented convertible with the top down. My music was turned up, and my hair was blowing in the wind. Basically, I was feeling good. One thing I want to note before continuing with this story is that this incident had happened several years before I met my boyfriend (aborted baby's father) and before the dreams of the little boy in heaven. As I proceeded to drive down the hill, I could see the oncoming traffic driving up the mountain toward me, going in the opposite direction. Then suddenly, I felt a swoosh of air move through my nose, as if someone had inserted a straw into my nose and taken a deep inhale, pulling the air from my nose. It felt like breath flew up and passed through one of my nostrils. Yes, I know this sounds crazy, but it really happened just that way. I honestly cannot explain it. A few seconds later, I could see in the distance, at the bottom of the hill, approximately two cars ahead of me, a black dog stepping off the sidewalk, attempting to cross the busy street, and a large van driving up the hill toward me. The driver failed to see the dog and, sadly, failed to stop to

72

allow the dog to cross the street. The poor dog was completely crushed under the van, and I could hear the dog cry one or two last yelps of sorrow and terror. By this point, I was so close to the van we were nearly parallel to each other, with our cars facing in opposite directions. I could hear the poor dog's bones breaking, and I started screaming at the van, "Please stop!" I was in utter shock. I was so angry and literally crying as I pressed hard on my car horn, trying to alert the driver of the van so he/she would stop.

However, my attempts to alert the driver of the van of the poor doggie failed, and the dog was killed right before my eyes. The sad thing is that had the van seen the dog and stopped, the next car that the dog would have walked in front of would have been mine. And its life would have been saved. I should note that I was driving a convertible with the top down, so for that reason, my ability to hear the dog was crystal clear.

There were two things that I noticed about the dog's fateful night. Number one, the dog was attempting to cross the street from the left side of the street (left of my vehicle) to the right side of the street, but it never made it. I am not sure what the significance of this moment was, but to this very day, I haven't forgotten it and still remember it as if it happened yesterday.

The second thing I could not help but notice was the event of the air swooshing through my nostrils moments before I saw and heard the poor dog screaming while being crushed under the van. This absolutely happened, and I'm still very confused about why or what the cold swooshing air moving through my nostrils actually was. But hindsight is twenty-twenty vision, and now I truly believe that the swoosh I felt move swiftly through my nostrils was the dog's soul leaving its body. I know this is hard to fathom, but it really happened: the events really, really happened just as I have described.

Somehow, God allowed me to experience this supernatural occurrence and the dog's soul moving through the air as it was being taken to heaven. Why God allowed me to experience this event is still a mystery to me. There are two scriptures in the Bible that support what happened this fateful night. The first is a verse from Genesis 2:7, "Then the LORD God formed man of the dust of the ground and breathed into his nostrils the breath of life, and man became a living soul."

The second scripture is Acts 1:9, "And when he had spoken these things, while they beheld, He [Jesus] was taken up; and a cloud received him out of their sight" (hereinafter, text in brackets added). These two scriptures support three things that happened that night. Number one, the fast cold upward-moving swooshing wind through my nostrils. Number two, every living thing has life, which is a living soul; hence, all life comes from God's soul. The soul exits the body the same way it enters the body: through the nostrils. When it leaves the body, it travels upward toward the clouds, apparently, moving through the air toward its destination. And not its final destination but a destination. I don't believe we will go to our final destinations until Yeshua returns. I have formed the above beliefs based on my supernatural experiences; I do not claim them to be true or based on any scientific factual evidence. Science still cannot explain God, nor will it ever be able to.

To this very day, I am not sure why I had this experience, but I did, and it was real. I could not make this up even if I wanted to because it is far too sad and deeply disturbing to my soul. And because of this experience, I do believe dogs, cats, and all animals and insects with living life in them will go to heaven when their flesh dies. I know this sounds far-fetched, but no one on this earth can say they know for sure as to the final destination of animals. No one has solved this mystery. And no one has solved the mystery of death. No one.

CHAPTER 4

THE SECOND SIGN: THE NUMBERS

Do Numbers Have Meaning?

November 22, 2011

*(44).

These numbers are still a mystery to me, and I still don't understand why they were sent to me. I still don't understand the meaning of these numbers. But I have come to believe that the number forty-four represents angels. All things that happened in my life were meant to happen as they did; thus, I know these numbers have a significant meaning.

Oh, My Goodness: a Supernatural Update to the Paragraph Titled "Do Numbers Have Meaning?"

Earlier, in what was originally written as a quick note in 2012, I wrote about the mysterious numbers

11/22/11 sent to me in 2012. The mysterious message or meaning of the numbers was not revealed to me in 2012.

In 2021, God sent the revelation of the numbers 11/22/11.

"Oh my God!" was all I could say as I sat completing the final edits of this book. On the morning of December 21, 2021, at approximately 2:25 a.m., while reading the passage regarding the mysterious meaning of the numbers 11/22/11, I paused in amazement and literal shock. Oh, my goodness, I had just spoken to my cousin on December 18, 2021, whom I hadn't spoken to in years. On December 18, 2021, I finally got the courage to speak to my cousin about her son, who had died many years ago, before I ever began writing this book. I never knew the actual date that he had died until I spoke to my cousin on December 18, 2021. Although I was around during the time of his death, I simply had forgotten the incident and all dates, days, or times associated with it. Upon speaking to me, she revealed his name and his date of death: November 23, 2011. I was in absolute awe when I began reading the paragraph on 11/22/11 in this book. Yes, the mystery of the numbers 11/22/11 had been revealed to me by Yeshua. I had no idea what those numbers meant until that very moment.

God is so real; the spirit world is so real. God is truly loving and miraculous.

Biblical Meaning of the Number Forty-Four

The period between Yeshua's (Jesus's) crucifixion and His ascension to heaven is reported as forty-four days: "And I will make thy seed as the dust of the earth: so that if a man can number the dust of the earth, then shall thy seed also be numbered" (Genesis 13:16). Forty-four is the number of chosen people. The number forty-four is birth and blood. So, the true chosen ones, the number forty-four (44), are closely linked to *the sons of light*, number twenty-two (22).

"While ye have light, believe in the light, that ye may be the children of light. These things spake Jesus, and departed, and did hide himself from them" (John 12:36).

The Hebrew alphabet is made up of 22 letters, which are used to compose the Word of God. The word of God is called a lamp (Psalms 119:105, Proverbs 6:22), thus it is the light by which we are to live.

"The Meaning of Numbers: The Number 22," Bible-study.org

It is important to remember that biblical numbers or numbers, in general, are usually described as having more than one meaning and/or association with a negative meaning or a positive meaning, depending on the situation. The word "God" appears 4,444 times in the King James Bible. The number forty-four had always appeared in my life when something great was about to happen.

"For many are called, but few are chosen" (Matthew 22:14).

The Meaning of the Number Eleven in the Bible

<2011>

Coming after ten (the number ten represents laws and responsibility), eleven represents the opposite; it represents the breaking of the law, which brings disorder and judgment.

Biblical Meaning of the Number Forty

Some believe that the number forty in the Bible means a period of testing, trial, or probation. I also see the number forty as symbolically connected to endings and beginnings. I have been writing this book for a number of years, primarily because of life obligations, such as work, family, etc. Refer to the Bible to see the various incidents that involved the number forty.

"Then Jesus was led up by the Spirit into the wilderness to be tempted by the devil. And when He had fasted forty days and forty nights, afterward He was hungry" (Matthew 4:1–2).

2020

At the start of 2020, I received a nudge from the Holy

Spirit saying, "Finish the book this year." At first, I wasn't sure if I actually heard a message from the Holy Spirit, but as the voice continued to repeat those words, "finish the book this year," I knew it was the voice of the Holy Spirit. Thus, I listened and sped up the process.

I couldn't help but notice the year 2020 was very interesting, to say the least. Numerically, if the two twenties are added together, they equal forty. I just find it very interesting that all of the events of this year seem to parallel some of the prophecies revealed in the book of Revelation in the Bible.

Abraham tried to bargain with God not to destroy Sodom and Gomorrah if forty righteous people were found (Genesis 18:29); God flooded the earth by having it rain for forty days and nights, and then the rain stopped (Genesis 7:12). The prophet Jonah powerfully warned ancient Nineveh that, in forty days, its destruction would come because of its many sins (Jonah 3:4).

Ironic Connection to the Number Twenty

The year 2020, I believe the majority would agree, was one of the worst years experienced by most human beings in history.

I just thought I would note that the number of children brutally murdered in the Sandy Hook massacre in 2012 was twenty.

2021

In January 2021, the voice of the Holy Spirit came again. This time the voice said, "Publish the book this year." Hence, I did not ask why; I just proceeded as instructed. However, I honestly believe there is a reason for the nudge because it is my belief that everything God does has a predestined purpose.

The Dreams: the First Dream

Jesus's visit to me came by way of a dream. It was the first dream of a series of dreams to come. And I believe it was the most important dream of them all.

This dream came on either October 23, 2012, or December 23, 2012. The original date written down by me was October 23, 2012. So, I honestly believe that was the date of the dream.

This dream is the most miraculous of all the dreams. In this dream, I was being led by an unseen angel. At least, I believe it must have been an angel guiding me. I could not see my guide in this dream, but I could feel the presence of the guide leading me through each part of the dream. This dream is the most amazing dream I have ever, ever, ever had in my life.

Jesus visited me in a dream; hence,

He knocked at my door.

I was in a community of people who were in need of help. The community appeared rife with bad doings. I didn't see the drugs in a direct form, but that was the mystery of the dream. I could feel that there were drugs and people addicted to drugs in the community. Then there were the drug dealers, two brothers: two handsome brothers. There was a male guide walking with me through the neighborhood. It was a large apartment community that was very, very clean looking. All the buildings were made of thick white concrete. A brilliant white that I truly cannot describe. I have never ever seen a white this brilliant on the earth. The material of the buildings appeared to be that of ancient wall stone, not wood.

I continued walking with the male guide, who spoke to me as we walked. While walking, he told me what I needed to do for one brother or what this brother wanted me to do. It should be noted that I could not see the face of the male guide; I could only hear his voice. The sky was sunny and blue. The apartment community appeared clean and filled with lots of people. I could hear their voices, but I could not see their faces. The guide instructed me to prepare a bowl of food for the brother who had called for me to serve him. I wanted to impress him, so I followed everything the guide told me to do. I walked alone to the left side of the guide. He led me through the village, but somehow, on occasion, I seemed to be walking along. I felt that my mission was to show or prove to one of the handsome brothers (the presumed drug dealer) that I could carry out his mission.

I had gathered the porridge or food in a bowl and was ready to take it to the man of my interest, but somehow, I found myself lying on my back, on the ground, in a field of green grass.

As I lay on the grass, looking up at the sky, I suddenly saw amidst the clouds a huge, long, dark cloud floating there. It was so large it practically looked like a huge float-ing *Titanic* ship with the bottom part visible to me. It didn't cover the entire sky, but it covered part of it. As I continued to look up at the sky, still lying on my back, I noticed the form of a man embedded in the cloud, and as I continued to look, I became astonished. It was Jesus. Jesus was in the cloud floating above the sky. His eyes were closed; His hair and beard were long and dark brown. He wore a long white garment. His arms were folded across the front of His body. He appeared to be lying flat on the cloud. His body was embedded in the cloud and stretched the entire length and width of the cloud.

I continued to stare at the cloud in awe, disbelief, won-der, and amazement. I wondered if I was really seeing what I thought I was seeing or if it was just a cloud with an apparent image of Jesus. Hum…several thoughts began running through my head: *Maybe it is just a cloud, and I am imagining things.* I was in absolute amazement, and still, to this very day, I continue to be in absolute amazement of this dream: it was so breathtaking and wonderful. So, I continued to look steadily at the image and then looked away to see if anyone else could see what I saw. I looked around the earth near me, frantically and happily, to see if anyone else could see what I could and if they were looking at the sky. But sadly, I didn't see anyone else near me. The city was dark; it was darkness all around me, and no one was watching, or at least no one appeared to be watching or looking at the sky or seeing what I thought I was seeing. In other words, I was the only one there, the only one watching. So, I returned my attention to the sky to see if Jesus was still there, surrounded by clouds. Yes, the humungous dark cloud was still there in the sky, and Jesus was still there in the middle of the cloud, floating above the earth, facing the earth, looking down at the earth. The best way for me to describe His position in the sky: picture yourself at the bottom of a pool, facing upward, and someone floating on top of the pool, facing downward toward you.

As I lay there on the grass, facing the sky, I still didn't believe that what I was seeing was real. I was in utter disbelief. How could this be and only I could see Him? Then suddenly, Jesus opened both of His eyes and appeared to wink or close His right eye as a way of confirming that I was really seeing what I thought I was seeing and that it was not just my imagination; it was really Him. Jesus's countenance appeared happy, peaceful, and cheerful. While in this dream, as I continued looking at the sky and at Jesus floating on the cloud, I smiled and felt tremendous peace inside.

Suddenly, my attention returned to the apartment community where I was. It was like I was again in the other scene of the dream, lying on the grass. I was back walking with the angelic guide who was previously guiding me through the community of buildings made of all white. We continued walking toward a set of stairs. There might have been two sets of stairs. Once we reached them, we began walking up the stairs to meet the handsome brother. I was carrying a bowl in my hands, and while walking, the guide asked me, "Have you met his brother?" I replied, "No." And suddenly, out of nowhere, came this second brother (sort of tall) walking with another, shorter man. They walked past us very quickly and didn't appear to notice us as they passed us very quickly, heading for the stairs. They came from behind our left side and reached the stairs before we did. They disappeared as they walked up the stairs.

Now, this second brother was originally thought to be handsome because of a vision I had of the brothers in the earthly realm. But as the dream continued, his true face was revealed, a face that was not attractive at all: his hair was braided back in cornrows, and his skin was filled with dark spots. I didn't notice the features of the other man with him. Also, the stairs they claimed did not appear to be the same stairs that my guide and I were approaching but rather a flight of stairs that were parallel to ours. However, this part of the dream is a bit faint, and for all intents and purposes, there might have only been one set of stairs.

Finally, my guide and I made it to the top of the stairs, and I handed the bowl of food to the handsome brother, who wore all white. He sat on a white concrete chair that appeared to have a tall back portion. He sat before me, appearing to be preoccupied, as he placed the bowl that I handed him down. I sat facing him, and he faced in my direction as well. I thought I was the only woman there when, suddenly, a beautiful light-skinned woman appeared sitting on my right side. She looked at me through a black veil, which completely covered her face, and said, "I am his wife." Then she said, "He was looking for another girl too." I looked at her and said, "I am a square, and I don't do things like that." She continued talking and looking in the direction of her husband when she suddenly lifted her legs, just slightly, to cross her feet. She was wearing black stilettos and a black dress. I noticed that she had beautiful legs and feet. Her hair was medium length and was blowing in the wind, underneath the black veil covering her face. One detail I almost forgot: I had on my red headscarf, which I removed so that my hair could blow in the wind as well. My hair was beautiful. I awoke from the dream. Also, I do believe my angelic guide was still there with the three of us but remained unseen.

Reflection on This Dream

While asleep, I was not afraid of Jesus when I saw Him. However, when I awoke, the dream was extremely frightening to me. I cannot explain why. But within moments, I felt complete peace and joy in my heart. A peace and joy that remains with me to this day.

The Second Supernatural Prophetic Movie

Meet Joe Black

<:>

One night, while watching television and randomly flipping through channels, I stumbled upon a movie titled *Meet Joe Black*, featuring Brad Pitt. And of course, since I am a lifelong respecter of Brad Pitt, I decided to watch the movie. Keep one thing in mind: I came across this movie completely unexpectedly, and shortly after, other supernatural experiences and occurrences began happening. Also, keep in mind that at the time all of this was happening, I had not yet started connecting the dots, nor was I aware that there was a puzzle or mystery unfolding and waiting to be solved. Therefore, I had no clue of what was really happening to me at all. Nor was I aware that I would later identify each of the aforementioned experiences as supernatural or prophetic experiences leading me to my God-given assignment.

Of course, I immediately fell in love with the movie because I love romance movies. Long story short, death decided to come to the earth in the form of flesh. Thus, death took on human form (entered into a man's body) and decided to walk the earth with a person whom death specifically selected for his mission. In this movie, death chose to visit a billionaire, whom he would later take away with him into eternity. However, initially, it was unbeknownst to the billionaire that his time to die was imminent. The very first thing death did was talk to the billionaire in spirit, meaning in an unseen fashion, to advise him that death was coming to pay him a visit and that his time to die would be coming soon.

Prior to manifesting in the flesh, death continued to whisper one word to the billionaire. That one word was "yes." The billionaire would be awakened from his sleep by the whispers of the word "yes." The second thing death did was reveal himself in the flesh to the billionaire. The way death revealed himself in the flesh was by taking on human form (he entered the body of a man). The third thing death did in the movie was that he answered the billionaire's question about his own death and whether his death was imminent. The final thing death did was he returned to his place, the spiritual dimension. Now, I know you are probably sitting there, scratching your head, wondering how this movie has any significance to my supernatural spiritual experience with the Lord.

1. God spoke to me through the spiritual voice (He sent signs and wonders) to advise me that death would be paying me a visit (my aborted son came to me by way of dreams). Hence this movie in and of itself was one of the signs.

2. God spoke to me through signs of things to come in the imminent future, wise men, dreams, visions, and physical manifestations by way of movies, pictures, documentaries, physical shadows, balloons, clouds, rainbows, steamy mirrors, messages from the church, and physical artifacts.

One thing I feel is always necessary is to reveal the connection of any statements made about God or the supernatural realm to similar occurrences in the Bible. Thus, in the Bible, Jesus sometimes used parables to reveal hidden truths to someone to whom he was speaking. He also used burning bushes (i.e., to speak to Moses):

> Now Moses kept the flock of Jethro his father in law, the priest of Midian: and he led the flock to the backside of the desert, and came to the mountain of God, even to Horeb. And the angel of the Lord appeared unto him in a flame of fire out of the midst of a bush.

Exodus 3:1–2

Thus, God has not changed. He continues to use several ways to get our attention when He needs it. Man cannot figure out God: He is an eternal mystery. Thus, it is called faith. It is called *believing*, and that is what one must do. One must believe, and one must have faith that God is.

CHAPTER 5

THE SECOND DREAM

The Stairs, the Sheep, the Red Heifer, and the Hidden Wolf

#;_;@%

In this dream, I was in a dimly lit area, very dark and smoky. Although I could not feel the temperature there, the room or area where I was standing had a very cold feeling about it. It was dark, gray, and foggy looking on the inside, definitely not a comfortable-feeling place. It was eerie and, quite frankly, scary. I stood there alone, looking at a black cast-iron spiral staircase that ascended straight up. The top of the staircase could not be seen because its ascension was very high; I estimated thirty or more stairs. I slowly began to walk up the stairs, heart beating fast, my mind wondering just what I might be walking into. But for some reason, I wasn't really afraid. To this day, even as I write these words, I still don't know why.

I continued slowly up the stairs and finally made it to the top. There was a small opening, somewhat like a small door through which I could look. I looked inside without actually putting my head through the door. What I saw was like something out of a scary old English fairytale. There was a humongous black cast-iron brewing pot, like the kind you would see in a witch's tale. There was steam blowing out of the top of the pot, which remained uncovered. And sitting to the right of the pot was a woman with a broom in her hand. She continuously dipped the broom into the pot, which appeared to be filled with very hot, boiling water. She used the broom as if it was a spoon to stir whatever was in the boiling water. She stirred as though she was pushing something down further into the pot, something she did not want to escape from her pot.

The woman had long gray hair and pale skin. She was not someone I would describe as attractive. Lying directly in front of the huge brewing pot on the floor was a heifer, red-orange in color, a red cow. I shifted my attention from the pot of boiling water to the heifer lying on the floor in front of the boiling pot. Somehow the word "heifer" came to mind as I peered at the animal. The heifer lay on its left side and had been pierced in its right side with a sword. The sword was impelled in the heifer's body and poked straight into its side. Within minutes, it became painfully clear that the cow had been killed and was about to be thrown into the pot of boiling water. I felt sadness run through my body as if I felt sorry for the heifer.

And before I could move or do anything, I looked to my immediate left, and there stood two frightened-looking sheep. They appeared to be lambs. They sat while the woman stirred the water. I believe there were actually two women sitting by the pot: one stirring and the other talking. They were talking to each other. The sheep were shivering as they looked on in silence and fear of the women.

I didn't know what to do. I stood there in absolute fear for the sheep and their inability to escape the terrible fate that appeared to await them. Somehow and suddenly, I decided to sneak up closer to the top of the stairs very quietly so as not to be seen by the two women, who resembled witches. I crawled up the stairs on my hands and knees and onto the floor underneath the huge pot barreling out steam into the ceiling. I was far enough away from the pot with boiling water and the women to successfully sneak into the room without being noticed. In hindsight, I thought it was also very miraculous that neither of the women ever noticed me. I quietly but quickly took hold of both of the sheep. I held one under my right arm and one under my left arm.

I carefully began scanning the room with my eyes, looking for an exit or escape. I found one. There was a door to the left of the room, down three stairs. I walked over to the door and pulled it slightly open. Before walking out of the door, I scanned the entire scene to be sure there were no witches outside waiting or watching me. When I felt it was safe to exit, I stepped outside the door with my left foot, to the point where the entire left side of my body was outside the door. The sheep in my left arm was also outside the door, under my arm. Then suddenly, I saw it. It was a wolf hiding in a bush. My face became filled with terror. The wolf appeared to be lying in wait for me to completely exit the door so that he could make his attack.

I was in such fear that my heart began racing and my legs began shaking. I quickly turned and tried to pull my body back inside the door while holding both sheep in each arm. I was in excruciating pain: my arms were burning from carrying the weight of both sheep. And just as I attempted to pull my body back inside the doorway of the dark, dingy room that appeared to be safer than what awaited us outside the door, the wolf lunged at me with a supernatural force and speed. He grabbed the sheep I held in my left arm by the neck and head and quickly ran off with it in his mouth. I was horrified. I had lost one of the sheep that I had been trying so desperately to save from the doom of the pot of boiling water. It all seemed to happen so fast: in the blink of an eye, he was gone with the sheep. And I awoke.

After awakening from the dream, I remember feeling relieved that it had only been a dream, or should I say, a nightmare, because there just didn't seem to be a win in that situation at all. I felt powerless against the evil that had snuffed out the life of the innocent, helpless little sheep. The dark dreariness of that house reeked of evil, and it was not a scary movie: it was terrifying; it was real;

it was nothing Hollywood could contrive.

The Third Supernatural Prophetic Movie

Nature

January 18, 2012

The History channel presented a documentary called *Nature*. This was a funny time in my life, but I had no idea of what was actually happening. I had no idea God was sending me messages and preparing me for what was to come.

Nature was a documentary about a mother leopard and her two cubs. In this episode, the mother leopard was tending to her normal duty of protecting and teaching her baby cubs how to survive in the wild. One of the leopard cubs wandered off into dangerous territory and had been completely separated from its mother. Meanwhile, there were several wild, hungry, angry baboons running around the jungle when one spotted the young leopard and immediately went on the attack after it. The baboon viciously pursued the young leopard and actually appeared to have caught it with its claws. There was a soft squeal-like scream coming from behind a large rock, where the baboon had chased the baby leopard who tried to hide. Within minutes, the baboon emerged from behind the rock victoriously, as to say it had successfully killed the cub. The saddest thing about this event, besides the fact that the baby cub died and was viciously killed, is that its mother and brother watched the whole event take place from their protective hiding spot. The end. Or was it?

Oh wait, the show had not actually ended. Several hours later, all of a sudden, the leopard cub emerged from its hiding spot. I thought it had been killed by the baboon. It emerged like a superhero for its mom and brother, quietly walking to rejoin them. Even the narrator of the show sounded surprised by the cub's emergence out of the rocks alive. When the cub reached its mother, the first thing it did was eat. Take note: it wanted its mother's milk, and it wanted the mother to feed it.

The Third Supernatural Prophetic Dream

I had a dream, a very short dream. In this dream, I heard a voice say, "Read page 131 in the book *The Kin of Ata Are Waiting for You* [originally titled *The Comforter*]."

Just a little background about this amazing book: when I was a student attending Alameda community college, one of my classes was taught by a substitute professor covering for the regular associate professor who was unable to teach the course for the semester. This professor looked a lot like he was straight out of Berkeley, California (i.e., Richard

Simmons with a blond curly afro). He taught the class in a very unorthodox fashion. The only text the students were assigned to read in his class was *The Kin of Ata Are Waiting for You*. This book and his class changed my life and my college experience. After I completed the course, the book never left my side.

When I opened the book to page 131, a very small passage at the top of the page read: "Her blue eyes stood out large in her thin face. 'Was I not there with you? Did I not jump into the fire with you when you called? I will always, always be with you when you call'" (Dorothy Bryant, *The Kin of Ata Are Waiting for You*, 131).

Augustine, the main character in the book, was still pregnant but very close to the Life Tree day; on that day, she would give birth to her baby. At the time of the dream, it was not clear as to why I was instructed to read this page of the book, but I knew, deep in my heart, there had to be something to it, a deeper meaning pointing me to a hidden supernatural truth. All I can say for now is ever since reading the book, I've always believed Ata was really heaven.

The Fourth Supernatural Prophetic Dream

The Second Child's Story

The Second Child in the Picture (in the Center)
/?\

2012

The First Dream of the Little Boy Wearing Red

When I fell into a deep sleep, I woke up in a house. No, I didn't really awake, but the dream was so vibrant it felt as if I was actually awake and sitting in a home on a large fluffy dark-green velvety couch. The couch was a deep-green leafy color. There were children playing. They were playing all over the house, laughing, and having fun. I sat on the couch, mentally watching them play. In other words, I couldn't actually see them with my physical eyes but could with the eyes of my mind, and I could hear their laughter very clearly. It was delightful listening to them play. It felt like there was also an adult in the home, but I could not see him or her at all.

The lighting in the room was a soft yellow, natural, comfortable lighting, not too bright and not too dark but perfectly balanced. As I sat on the huge, extremely soft, comfortable couch, I suddenly looked down to my left, and there was one child, a little baby boy, approximately three or four years old, sitting next to me. His hair was a soft golden-red color and curly in texture. He wore a red onesie jumper with white bottoms on the feet. He sat on my left side, swinging his feet backward and forward the way a child would if sitting on a large chair or couch where their feet could not completely touch the floor. He did not speak but sat quietly, swinging his legs back and forth in a jolly way.

I sat looking at him and talking to him. I didn't know where I was, but I was extremely comfortable and at ease. The house felt so cozy and warm. He never spoke using words, but his energy was amazing. I've always loved the cuteness of children. And he just sat there, swinging his little legs back and forth. His skin was a warm honey color; his eyes were almond-shaped, and his mouth was a bit eccentric with a small upper lip and slightly larger bottom. He was very cute, but it was his jolly happy spirit that stood out the most to me. Time was of no concern: we just sat there on the couch side by side the whole time. He never spoke a word.

And then suddenly, while I was looking at him, trying to talk to him, he jumped off the couch and started running fast toward the front door of the house. My eyes popped out of my head, and I could feel my heart racing. It was so sudden that he arose and began running for the front door. I thought, *Maybe he has decided to join the other children playing in the home.* Again, I knew there were other children there because I could hear them. I could not see them but could hear their laughter. But I wasn't ready for him to run away: I had begun to take a liking to him. Well, that combined with the idea that I simply didn't know what was on the other side of the door that he was approaching. *But obviously*, the thought crossed my mind, *if we are in a house and there is a door in the front of the house, it must lead outside. Inside the house, it is safe for him, but outside…Hum, I just don't know what is out there. It can be cars with streets and danger.*

I jumped up, sort of clumsily, because I had gotten pretty relaxed on the nice comfy couch. I chased him, running as fast as my body would move, yelling, "Stop, please stop, kid, stop!" I didn't know his name, so all I could yell was, "No, no, no, child, stop! Please stop." With my right arm extended outward in his direction, I continued yelling, "Don't go there!" But to no avail: I could not stop him from running. Suddenly, he pushed the door, and it easily flung open. I couldn't figure out how he managed to open the door with such ease. I'm still not sure if he opened it or went through it. Nevertheless, he made it out to the other side. And there, in front of the home, was grass and a chain-link fence around the house.

And I still don't know why I looked up to my left, but it was good I did because there was a humongous red diesel truck approaching the child as he neared the street. I began screaming in horror for the little boy to stop. He didn't hear me, nor did he respond to my requests for him to stop. He kept running, laughing, and smiling in a childlike manner until he reached the center of the street. The driver of the truck looked at me (I think), but he didn't see the child who appeared to be headed for an inevitable fate, one I so desperately wanted to save him from.

The moment seemed to last no longer than the blink of an eye. I was too late. I could not save him. The truck came to a sliding, screeching halt only after it had completely crushed the child. I was horrified; I couldn't believe what had just happened. Although I watched the truck run over the child, the literal view of the child's crushed body or the sound of him screaming was shielded from me. The little boy was lost. The child was lost; he died. I couldn't believe it: this beautiful baby was brutally killed, and worse of all, I could not save him. He ran so fast that I (the protector) could not save him from this terrible fate. I could not bear the pain of the sight of the truck running over the baby or of this terrible dream, and within a moment, I violently shook my body out of this nightmare.

Have you ever had such a bad dream, a nightmare, which was so profound that when you awoke, you felt a sigh of relief and comfort to know that it was only a dream? Yes, that is how I felt.

I was so happy that it had only been a dream that when I awoke, I made the following statement, "God, what kind of dream was that?" In other words: Why would God let me have such a dream as that? It was awful. I probably hadn't spoken God's name in eons, but in the moment that I shook myself out of that dream, it was a natural instinct to want to turn to God and ask, "Why, God? Why *that* dream?"

CHAPTER 6

THE FIFTH SUPERNATURAL PROPHETIC DREAM

Second Dream of the Little Boy Wearing Red

Another dream came just days after the first horrific dream of the little boy being run over by the diesel truck. I found myself sitting in the exact same position, on the exact same couch, in the exact same house. Suddenly, I looked down to my right, and there was the same little boy sitting next to me, wearing the same red onesie jumpsuit. He was swinging his legs backward and forward, just like in the first dream. He was smiling and appeared happy, just as he was in the first dream. The only difference was that in the first dream, he was sitting on my left side. In this dream, he was sitting on my right side. Wow.

I continued to stare at him. He didn't have one scar or bruise anywhere on his body. He was completely intact, whole, and normal-looking. I sat there, looking at him in disbelief and shock. My mouth was wide open, and my eyeballs were popping out of their sockets. I couldn't take my eyes off him.

Finally, when my heart stopped pounding in sheer joy and excitement, I turned to him and said, "But you, um, you, ah, kind of—" I didn't know how to finish my sentence. "Uh, how are you still here? You were in a horrible accident, but you don't appear hurt."

He did not respond. Maybe he didn't understand what I was saying because he was still just a little baby boy. The other difference was that this time, I could hear other children laughing and playing but could not see them mentally as I could in the first dream. I could hear them laughing and playing in another section of the house, but they could not be seen at all. So, I looked down at the little boy and asked, "Why are you sitting here with me? Don't you want to join the other children playing?" Again, he did not respond. He just sat there, swinging his feet back and forth while smiling. He was absolutely adorable and happy. Somehow, he gave me a sense of peace and joy inside. How could he have survived such a horrible accident? I was so happy for him that he actually survived. Suddenly, he turned to look at me (for the first time) and tilted his head backward with his mouth open. I didn't understand what he was doing or what he was trying to say. *Hum*, I said in my mind while thinking, *What does he want?*

Note: remember the leopard cub in the second documentary. Was this documentary a premonition of the dreams to come?

The Hand in the Fifth Dream

And then, out of nowhere, a hand that was slightly above us appeared, holding a bowl. The hand gently reached in and handed me the bowl with a spoon and food in it. Initially, while looking at the hand, I was bewildered and confused. *What is this?* I sat, thinking. *Whose hand is this, and what am I supposed to do?* I looked back at the child, with his head still tilted backward and his mouth opened, facing me. *Oh, okay, I get it,* and within a moment, I figured it out. *He wants me to feed him; he is hungry.* Maybe it was time for him to eat. So, I gladly began to feed him, and yes, he was very hungry. He ate the whole bowl of what appeared to be Cream of Wheat or something similar.

The hand disappeared instantly after handing me the bowl. The little baby never said a word; he just ate and sat, swinging his feet happily.

The person who handed me the bowl never appeared or revealed himself or herself to me. The only thing I could see was the hand. It was a human hand. I was so confused but happy to see that the baby boy had been saved and that everything had worked out for him. This dream was much happier than the first one and ended on a much happier note, with the baby being fed. I was so happy for him and the happy ending. At least, I thought it was the end of the story.

Now that I sit writing, I remember there was a story just as mysterious—the only other time I know of where there's a hand performing a task without a body attached to it.

Notation: Remember the second real-life documentary with the leopard cub that was attacked by the baboon? After the cub's traumatic incident, the very first thing it did upon returning to its mother was eat.

Correlations with the Bible: the Hand in the Bible

The story of King Belshazzar's "hand" and the writing on the wall.

This Bible story was revealed to me six years after the dreams of Christopher. One day, while listening to Rabbi Schneider on Daystar television, I learned this story.

Belshazzar, the king, made a great feast for a thousand of his lords and drank wine before the thousand. Belshazzar, while tasting the wine, commanded the servants to bring the golden and silver vessels, which his father, Nebuchadnezzar, had taken out of the temple located in Jerusalem; "that the king and his princes, his wives, and his concubines might drink therein" (Daniel 5:2). Then they brought the golden vessels that had been taken (stolen) out of the temple of the house of God in Jerusalem. The king and his princes, his wives, and his concubines drank of them.

They drank wine, and praised the gods of gold, of silver, of brass, of iron, of wood, and of stone" In the same hour came forth fingers of a man's hand and wrote over against the candlestick upon the plaster of the wall of the king's palace: and the king saw the part of the hand that wrote. Then the king's countenance was changed, and his thoughts troubled him, so that the joints of his loins were loosed, and his knees smote one against another.

Daniel 5:4–6

This is the only other time I have heard of a hand magically appearing without a human body attached to it in my entire life. Shortly after the hand appeared to King Belshazzar, writing a message of doom on the wall, Belshazzar's kingdom was destroyed—that same night (Daniel 5:30).

The Sixth Supernatural Prophetic Dream

The Third Dream of the Little Boy Wearing Red

And then there was the third (recurring) dream of the little boy wearing the red onesie. In the first two dreams, he was wearing red; however, in this third dream, he was wearing blue jeans and a striped shirt. The stripes were thick, blue, and horizontal. This time he was not alone.

He was with my living son, Donovan, and my boyfriend's living daughter, Special K. (real names deliberately concealed). Another thing I noticed in this dream was that I could still hear the laughter of other children in the house. Seemingly, there were many children in the house playing; however, like in the first two dreams, I could not see them. Unlike the first two dreams, this time, I could also hear the laughter of the little baby boy who was sitting next to me. Not only could I see him and hear his laughter, but I could also see and hear the laughter of Special K. and Donovan.

All three of them were running through the large house, which appeared to have many rooms like that of a mansion. I couldn't see the other rooms physically, but I could see them with my mind. The trio kept running in a playful manner in and out of several rooms of the house. They were all running and playing together, laughing and having fun. One thing I noticed was that I was not running with them; I could see them with my mind, but I wasn't physically next to them. I was sitting on the same large green couch by myself.

And then, the three of them ran into a large bedroom where my stepbrother, Charles, was sleeping. Until this very day, I cannot figure out why Charles was in this dream, but he was. When they ran into his room, they were still laughing and playing and accidentally awoke him. He awoke angrily and yelled for them to leave his room immediately. In a playful frenzy, the three kids ran out of his room. Of course, Special K. and Donovan were running way ahead of the little baby boy wearing the striped shirt because he was a lot younger and smaller than them. While running out of Charles's room, Special K. led the pack, Donovan was second, and the little baby boy was last. Running behind the two, the baby boy tripped and accidentally fell down onto his knees, but within a second, he pushed himself back to his feet and continued running behind the other children. And suddenly, the trio was standing in front of me, in the room where I was sitting on the couch. The three of them approached me, still breathing heavily from all the playing and running they were doing. Special K. was standing on the right side of the baby boy, and Donovan was standing on his left side.

And suddenly, out of nowhere, Special K. looked at me and said, "Taylor, this is my brother."

I responded to her, "What?"

She replied again, "This is my brother."

I looked at her, perplexed, because her dad and I had been together for the last seven years. So, it would be impossible (I thought) for him to have a baby son who was so young and much younger than his daughter, who was already at least two years old when we met.

"How old is he?" I looked at her and asked.

She responded, "Five."

I looked at the boy and asked him, "Is she your sister?"

He just looked at me and didn't respond. I asked him

again, as nicely as I could, considering I was beginning to get nervous and a bit upset at the idea of my boyfriend fathering another child outside of our relationship. All kinds of thoughts started running through my head as I sat there, becoming increasingly angry at the idea of the little boy being her brother and of Mr. N. having another child.

My heart was beating fast, and my mind was foggy, sort of like the body's physical response when a person is about to have a physical altercation. The prefrontal cortex in the brain shuts down when a person goes into fight-or-flight mode. *How can this be?* I thought simultaneously. *How can Mr. N. have a son? A very young son, approximately age four or five.* Mr. N. and I had been together for almost seven or eight years, so, if he was the father of a child of approximate age four or five, that could only mean one thing: he fathered a child outside of our relationship. Yes, that would mean he had cheated on me and gotten a woman pregnant during the affair. So, that would make this cute little boy his love child of an extra relationship outside of ours.

I sat there fuming as I looked at the children, trying to hold back my anger, for it was not the baby with who I needed to be angry. I immediately jumped off the couch and ended up in another room where Mr. N. was sitting on a couch alone. How I knew he was in another room in the house or where to find him remains a mystery to me to this very day.

The trio (Special K., Donovan, and the baby boy wearing the striped shirt) followed closely and silently behind me. And there he was; I ran straight at him, yelling and screaming, "You cheated on me!" I was going crazy, yelling and screaming at him. He sat there, looking perplexed and confused while holding his arms and hands straight in the air. He sat there thinking and trying to remember how he could have another child, looking confused and bewildered.

I watched him closely while he sat thinking. While sitting, looking at the ceiling, hand on chin, he finally spoke out with, "Oh, I think it could have been my office secretary, um, well, um, you know." My face turned red-hot as I lunged at him. I began screaming and hitting him in the face repeatedly. I never gave any thought to the three children standing behind me, watching in horror. I'm not sure how long my yelling and screaming lasted.

Mr. N. just sat there, staring at me. He appeared to be at a loss for words. It seemed as though he was trying to figure out how he could have fathered a child during our relationship. The three children stood there looking just as shocked and confused. One thing I noted was that I could no longer hear the laughter of the children in the background. I couldn't hear anything anymore but myself screaming and fighting. This dream was so horrible, so real, so devastatingly horrible that I literally couldn't take it anymore. I could feel myself kicking my feet (in real life) as I lay in my bed. I was not kicking as if I was fighting Mr. N.; I was kicking as if I was fighting myself, fighting to get out of what started as a dream and quickly turned into a nightmare. I kicked until suddenly I could feel myself sitting straight up in the bed. Whew, I was awake, fully awake, as I felt myself pushing my body upward.

As I sat reflecting on the dream (i.e., nightmare) I had just awakened from, I began feeling horrible inside because I had acted so terribly in front of the three children. My behavior was somewhat typical of how I might have responded in real life after receiving that kind of news: belligerent and ignorant, lacking any temperance or control. I literally awoke myself by forcing my body to move; though I was in a deep sleep, I needed to escape the embarrassment and horror I was causing to myself and the children.

I was so happy to be awake. As I sat there thinking of the nightmare I had just awakened from, I was breathing hard, as if I had literally just been involved in a fight, a real fight. I sat on my bed for at least an hour, reflecting on this dream. My thoughts were racing, and I was so confused. Why would I have such a terrible dream? Why had I erupted with such anger and violence in front of three innocent children, without any regard for them? I sat there thinking, *What is up with these weird dreams?*

An Important Correlation of the Sixth Dream

This is just a sidenote for reflection. There is no word for "irony" or "coincidence" in the Hebrew Bible. Sometime either before or after I had the third dream of the little boy initially wearing a red onesie and later wearing the blue striped shirt and jeans, I discovered a picture my alive son, Donovan, had drawn for me. I don't know when he drew it or when he gave it to me. Somehow, incidentally and without searching, I just stumbled upon it well after I had all the dreams.

I believe the picture Donovan drew was meant to be a picture of him and me, but as I said before, God works in very mysterious ways, and He can speak through a child without the child ever knowing that He is sending a message through them.

Notice: in the picture below, a little boy is standing next to me on my right side. In the first dream, where the little baby boy died, he sat next to me on the couch to my left. In all of the remaining dreams, he sat next to me to my right.

GOD'S ANSWER TO ABORTION

When the puzzle of the supernatural dreams, visions, miraculous events, signs, and wonders started coming together, I began looking at everything differently and through a supernatural lens. And that is when I began to see everything clearly. Now, keep in mind: my son Donovan was also present in the third dream that I had of the little boy in heaven. In the third dream, the little boy was wearing a shirt with blue horizontal stripes, exactly as shown in the picture above. Also, in the picture above, the little boy is standing on my right side, the same as depicted in my second dream of him, where he appeared sitting next to me on my right side.

Correlation with the Bible

When Jesus ascended to heaven, He sat at the right side of God's throne (Mark 16:19). Right appears to mean the third heaven. The words on Donovan's picture read, "Love Mom." What does this all mean? Is it irony or coincidence that my son would draw a picture of a child (presumably meant to be himself) and me with himself wearing an outfit identical to that of the little boy depicted in my third dream?

I believe God, Jesus, and the Holy Spirit can move through all earthly beings as they choose and without limitation. In the Bible, this is depicted on several occasions. Somehow, Donovan drew a picture of the little boy in heaven without knowing what he was doing. God used him to show me that the dream I had had of the little boy was real.

In hindsight, I do recall that after each dream or vision, some form of a physical manifestation occurred. Manifestations like pictures, cards, movies, artifacts, heavenly sightings, or something in the physical realm supported the authenticity of the dream or vision that either occurred in the heavenly realm or was sent from the heavenly realm. Isn't God nice? He wanted me to know that I was not a fool and that I was not crazy.

Heaven Is for Real!

Remember the movie *Heaven Is for Real*? God used the earthly brother of the little girl who was in heaven to send a message from her (his sister) in heaven to their mother on the earth. The little boy had never met his sister in the earthly realm, only in the heavenly realm. The fact that he knew he had a sister in heaven astonished his mother because he was not told that the mother had had a daughter who had gone to heaven by way of a miscarriage. This movie was based on a true story. Note this movie wasn't produced until 2014. At the start of my dreams and supernatural experience, this movie didn't exist. I personally didn't come across this movie until sometime in 2019.

Continued Reflections

As I continued sitting on my bed after awakening from the third dream, I continued thinking, *Who is the little boy in my dreams? And why or how can it be that I am encountering the same little boy in multiple dreams?*

How was this possible if dreams were random and most times not repeated, at least not for me? Not only that, but also this mysterious house filled with the laughter of children whom I could not see. A house that felt so warm, beautiful, bright, and spacious. There were so many rooms that I'm sure I had not seen all of them. Actually, I had only really been in one room, well, two in all of the dreams: the first room where I originally met the little baby boy wearing the red onesie and the second room where Mr. N. was sitting when I began fighting him. The other rooms where Donovan, Special K., and the little boy wearing a blue striped shirt had been running and playing were only seen in my mind, but I was not physically present with them as they ran and played. And why had I not been allowed to see the other children in the home? Why was I allowed to hear their laughter and cheer but not allowed to see them physically? And even when I felt as if I could see them in my mind, I don't believe I really saw any faces, just glares of color.

And why had Special K. called the little boy her brother and not Donovan? And why is it that Special K. had been the child chosen to speak to me and reveal that the little boy was her brother? I mean, honestly, in real life, Special K. and I rarely spoke at all. If the dream had been of my making, I definitely would have chosen Donovan, my son, to speak to me in the dream. The mystery and answers to these questions would later be revealed to me, but I will not reveal them in this book. Maybe, should we ever meet, I will reveal it to you.

This was all so surreal. And had Mr. N. really cheated on me? I was so confused as to why these dreams were appearing so real, so vivid as if I had actually physically been in the dreams and the home for real. And each time I awoke from the dreams, my heart was beating faster and my breath felt heavier. This dream was so real; I mean, both of our children were there: Donovan (my alive son) and Special K. (Mr. N.'s alive daughter) appeared in this dream. And with them was the mystery child, the cute cheerful little boy wearing the red onesie in my previous dreams.

In the dream, Mr. N. appeared to have fathered the cute little baby boy with someone else. Judging from the age of the child, I guessed he would have fathered this child during the time he and I had been together in our relationship, during the initial stages of our relationship, maybe like the first or second year. There were so many questions. And why had my brother, Charles, been in my dream? I hadn't spoken to him in years, and out of nowhere, he appeared in my dream.

As if all of the above wasn't enough. Go figure: this would not be the last dream of the little boy wearing red in some dreams and a blue-and-white striped shirt in others.

I sat on my bed feeling like there must be some truth to the dreams. Maybe God was trying to reveal Mr. N.'s affair to me, and maybe I needed to investigate things further. I sat there reflecting on my life with Mr. N., our long-term relationship, and our roller-coaster lifestyle, *Hum, and now all these crazy dreams, hum, why? Why am I having these dreams?*

Not just dreams, but dreams of the same baby boy, dreams of Jesus, dreams of witches, wolves, a red heifer, boiling pots, scary stairs, two crazy brothers, and some of these dreams were more like nightmares. Not to mention the funny image on my bathroom mirror one morning as I prepared for work. I sat thinking, pondering, *What is the likelihood of me dreaming of the same child in multiple different dreams in rapid succession?* I have heard of people having reoccurring dreams, but my dreams were not necessarily the same reoccurring dream but rather multiple different dreams in different scenes, with the same child in all of them.

I continued sitting there on my bed, totally confused and a bit bewildered. What was happening to me? After several minutes, maybe even an hour, had passed, I began reflecting on all the other dreams of the little baby boy.

How in the world was the same baby boy appearing to me in multiple dreams? And the mysterious hand that reached in and handed me a bowl of food to feed him. Why was there only a hand and not a person attached to it? Using my most colloquial language, I said out loud, "What the heck is going on?"

After the dreams began, I continued experiencing crazy thoughts, dreams, signs, visions, real-life experiences, sighting, finding heavenly artifacts, and mysterious cards: one that was sent to me by mail and the other I mysteriously stumbled upon.

CHAPTER 7

BUT FIRST, THE THOUGHTS

Thoughts, thoughts, thoughts were running through my head as I lay on my bed, trying to figure out my dreams and why I had been having so many strange dreams of the same place and the same child. I just couldn't make sense of it all.

I let out a sigh, "Shucks."

I was so preoccupied with my life consisting of immoral sex, drugs, and all things ungodly that there was simply no time to think of anything or anyone else. I mean, I had always loved and believed in God and Jesus, but this was not the particular time in my life to have a covenant relationship with the Lord God or Jesus. I simply wasn't thinking of God or Yeshua every day at this time in my life. I still can't figure out why Yeshua took an interest in me at all.

I mean, I was living more like a street woman running wild than a saint. I always thought God only came to special, chosen people whom He had set aside as His own. However, based on my supernatural experience, I can tell you this is not true at all. How God chooses people to use for His purposes is a mystery to me.

As I began contemplating moving from my bed to the floor, where I would continue lying down, I experienced a Eureka moment. I began thinking back on my relationship with Mr. N., and my mind took me to the very beginning of our relationship when we first started dating. We were wild and having nonstop fun as new lovebirds. And then, after reflecting on my life and all the dreams, it hit me like a brick in the head.

I began shouting out, "Wait, wait, wait, wait! That's it, that's it! I—" and after a long pause, I finished, "I...think I remember having an abortion." Thinking and talking out loud to myself, "That's it: I had an abortion," I began frantically walking around my room. I got up and ran into the living room, where Mr. N. was sitting. I shouted, "N., do you remember me having an abortion?" He looked up at me in a matter-of-fact way and replied, "I don't know," while shrugging his shoulders as if he was a bit bothered by the question or by my interrupting him. But I was immediately excited; I was perturbed; I was bothered by the idea that I couldn't even really remember the incident or even having an abortion because it had meant so little to me when I did it.

I continued pondering the event, and suddenly, it all began coming back to me. "Yes, N., we had an abortion. Don't you remember?" I continued to try to spark a flame in him; I wanted him to validate me, to validate that he, too, had had an abortion with me because he had approved of it. As usual, he didn't give much attention to me while I was speaking, but finally, he looked up at me and replied, "Yes, I think you did." Hum, me? He was placing blame for the abortion squarely on me and recusing himself. Well, I was horrified by the idea that we were both so selfish, so callous, so…inhumane that we could barely remember having the abortion because it meant nothing to us. After thinking very hard about the situation, I calculated that the abortion had to have taken place about five or seven years prior.

The light in my head finally went on. The light was so luminous I was blinded by it. The little boy in the dream had not been the love child of Mr. N. with another woman or of an affair. I was the woman; the woman was me. I shouted out loud, "It was me; it was me; I am the mother. I am the mother, he, um…he…is my son, my son, my son, and Mr. N., yes, N. is the father."

I instantly collapsed to the floor on my face and knees. I begin to weep bitterly, inconsolably. For hours, I continued crying and sobbing so loud and so hard I could feel my body trembling. I spent the rest of the day weeping. I was lying in a pool of tears, misery, and remorse for what I had done and for not knowing that what I had done was wrong and, obviously, meant something to God and Yeshua, even though it meant absolutely nothing to me. Nothing at all. I couldn't believe what was happening to me; this was some kind of craziness. I can't even describe in words how I felt in that moment.

Now it all made sense: the dreams, the visions, the nudging, and subtle sightings of hearts, sparkles, and things that I had been so oblivious to. That is until this day, this moment, and the third dream of the child, the boy, my son in heaven. I cried out loud while sitting on my knees, "God, Jesus, please forgive me, for I am a fool; I did not know what I was doing; I did not know, for I know not what I do." This begging and crying and talking to God, Jesus, and the Holy Spirit went on and on for several hours, days, and nights thereafter. I couldn't stop thinking of everything.

I continued weeping uncontrollably for several hours that day because I could not stop the pain of the realization of what happened, how it happened, and what I had done. I had killed my own child, my son, my baby, and mercilessly taken an innocent life. How could I? How could I do this to a child? How could I do this to God? How could I do it? It was all so surreal to me, so deep, too deep, and the wound I felt in my heart cut deep. I literally could not push my limp body off the floor; I couldn't believe what I had done, and most importantly, that he came back to me through the realm of the Holy Spirit and at the beckoning of the Lord Jesus. How else could I be experiencing something so supernatural, so amazing, and so out of this world? It had to be God: there is simply no other way to explain it.

As I sat there kneeling, crying, and sobbing, I cried out in a loud voice, "Lord, please, I owe it to him to never forget him. Please, God, I never want to forget his face; please, God, I pray: let him come again, let him come back to me again. I never want to forget his face. I will never forget him again. Lord, please, never let me forget his face. It is the least I can do. I couldn't give him life, but please, God, have mercy on me, have mercy on my soul, and grant that I never forget his face."

I was completely discombobulated, mentally overwhelmed by it all. And, rightfully so, I deserved no peace. I began working through it all in my mind, trying to figure out what I could do to capture my child's face and keep it with me forever in this world since it was blatantly clear that he was now residing in the third heaven with God and would never be able to return to me or this earth. I began losing it again, shouting out loud, "I killed him, I killed him." Bent on hands and knees, I began crying out, holding my face in my hands. There simply are not enough pages in this book to capture exactly how long this miserable scene lasted.

For whatever stupid reason, I didn't think I would get pregnant, so Mr. N. and I engaged in unprotected sex when we first met. We barely knew each other. I continued speaking out loud, talking to myself, "I remember how it all happened now. I remember now, I remember now. Yes, now I remember." Thinking back on that day, the day of the abortion, I recollected Mr. N. was a very, very willing participant in the abortion. He was wearing a red hoodie sweatshirt the day of my abortion. He drove me to the abortion clinic and waited for me until the procedure was completed. After it was completed, I could tell he was relieved.

And I know that God, Lord Jesus, had not sent my son to me to make me miserable but that the natural result of sin is misery. How could I not be, after God lifted the veil from my eyes? As I sat there, I shut my eyes tight and began reflecting on all the dreams I had had prior to this morning, and everything started making a lot more sense. It was all coming back to me now. The day, the clinic. *The clinic, the clinic, the clinic, the clinic? Oh no, I must go there to get my paperwork; he deserves at least for me to know the day he died and the day he was born into heaven.*

My son was a human, who lived, he *lived*, I say, he lived and died on this earth, in my womb, and he deserved for someone to know that he had lived, that he was human, that he was beautiful, that he, too, was a child; he was a baby; he was a life; flesh or not, he was alive, and I killed him, I let him die. I needed to know the day he died. I had to know. This morning, this day was the first day of the rest of my life. I knew from that moment that day my life would never be the same again. How could my son be so happy in the dreams? How could he love me still? How could he? And most importantly, how could I?

I prayed to God to never remove the dreams from the vision of my mind, to never let me forget his face, and to help me find him, to find his record of life. I sat there thinking of the first thing I needed to do. I would go to Venice Beach and hire a street artist to draw a picture of him based on the description I would provide. He was a honey complexion with red curly hair. His eyes were almond-shaped like mine. His mouth was shaped like mine. He was a beautiful baby; he was a beautiful child. How could I do it? How could I? And to think of his beautiful face in the dream and how he sought after me with such love, with such peace, and such a beautiful, loving smile each time I saw him in all of the dreams. He embraced the person who had murdered him with agape love. And still, he loved me. Until this very moment, I cry when I think of his innocent face: so loving, so kind. The next thing I would have to do is go to that awful place, the clinic, and leave flowers on his grave, the only grave site I gave him. And again, I began weeping inconsolably.

The Holy Spirit (something I never gave any thought to before) descended on me and created an open portal to heaven. The portal, which opened without me actually dying in the flesh, allowed me a rare view into the supernatural world of heaven. My aborted son, whom I had aborted approximately five to seven years ago, came to me in dreams, several dreams.

But why and how? I mean, how did he find me or know I was his mother? This was all too much for me, way too much. I mean, I felt like I was going crazy, and I was afraid everyone would think I was going crazy as well if I told them of my dreams and supernatural experiences.

I spent the rest of the week trying to figure out how to get my abortion records from Planned Parenthood and how to get an artist to capture the image held in my heart and head of the little boy I dreamed of. I would make it my mission never to forget him or his face.

I began making calls to various Planned Parenthood clinics, trying to figure out how to get my records, detailing the date and time of the abortion. I had literally forgotten the exact location of the clinic, I mean, I had a general idea, but the memory of it all was really foggy. I needed to know the exact date so that I could give this date a meaning, the true meaning it deserved: the day marking the death of my son. First, I tried to call the clinic in Venice, where I believed I actually had the abortion. I soon discovered this clinic had been shut down. So, I continued making calls to other Planned Parenthood clinic locations to see if I could somehow retrieve the vital information that I was seeking. And each time, I was given the same answer from them: all records of abortions are deleted after five years post the abortion. I couldn't believe it: How could they delete the records, such important medical information? But apparently, records of human life and death simply weren't that important to them. I tried to no avail; I was not able to get the records or any solid answers as to why the records were destroyed after five years. So, for now, it seemed that the only record I would have of the abortion and of my son's death, besides my boyfriend's account of it, would be that remaining in my heart and mind forever.

Return to the Abortion Clinic, My Son's Only Grave

:...(

After all the dreams of the little baby boy in heaven, my son, I knew I had to go back: I had to go to the location where he died. It felt urgent that I do so; it was the least I could do for him, and it was the only thing that I could do for myself.

Yes, I would go to the awful place where my son died and leave some balloons and flowers for him, for his memory, for his love, the love he sent me from heaven. The love that let me know he was all right and that I would be all right, too, until I see him again. So, later that week, I mustered up the courage to drive to the clinic where he died. I cried the whole time during the drive. As I drove, the dreams kept running through my mind: his face, his body, his smile, his hair, his happy spirit. But I deliberately blocked the worst dream out of my mind, the dream where he had been crushed to death by the truck. The awful red truck. As I finally arrived at the clinic's location, I slowly pulled up to park and was instantly startled by what I saw. I couldn't believe the sight before my eyes.

I slowly got out of my car and walked up to what now stood as a dark, abandoned building with tall, dry yellow weeds and tares completely covering the property. The weeds grew up the walls of the edifice, where green ivy had once been. A building that was once deceptively beautiful and opulent was now no more than a pile of intertangled weeds and dead grass. There was no sign of life there. The building was surrounded by a dilapidated broken-down chain-linked fence erected to protect the property from outsiders. The site was dark, eerie, and looked like a graveyard without all its previous fancy beautifications. Ironically, the gray darkness looming over the abortion clinic reminded me of the gray darkness of the witches' dwelling place in one of my previous dreams: the dream with the spiral staircase leading up to a dark room where two women who looked like witches sat on the sides of a large dark cast-iron pot. The dark thick gray air that circulated through the witches' dwelling place like a thick fog blocking all visibility was instantly vivid in my mind as I stood at the gate, looking through the holes in the fence. I felt like I was back there in that nightmarish dream again. That is how the clinic felt as I stood there crying, looking through the gate.

I can't really describe in words the eerie feeling circulating throughout the entire property, but it can be best described as feeling like a place where death loomed. Like a cursed place. The gate was locked with a double-thick chain equipped with a huge bolt to keep trespassers from entering the property. The look of the surrounding outside area was like that of a haunted house that you might see in a horror movie: gray, dreary, drab, dark, with a smoky mist moving throughout the property. The windows of the building were covered with cobwebs and thick-looking dirt and debris. The windows were so dark they appeared tinted so that no one could see inside. Although the place was huge and formally very beautiful and pleasing to the eye, that day, it was no more than a gloomy graveyard that had taken the lives of many innocent souls. If I were to estimate the approximate number of babies that were slaughtered there, it would be hundreds of thousands.

As I held onto the fence with clenched hands, as if I was holding on for dear life, crying, I forced myself to walk away. I couldn't take it anymore. I had to get away from that place. It was death, pure death, so hurtful, so painful as I sat there, visualizing all the cries of the babies dying there.

A Bit of What Felt like a Forced Dream

<<<<<<<[*} >>>>>>>

Ever wanted something so bad that you could force your mind to make it manifest?

133

I wanted to dream of him (my son in heaven) again so bad that I spent days thinking of him. And then it happened (and very unexpectedly): I had another dream of the little boy in heaven. But this dream felt somewhat like a forced dream: as if I forced my mind to create it.

In this dream, my son was floating around in space. There were all sorts of pictures and images floating around with him. These appeared to be toys. There was another little boy with him, floating around. The other little boy wore his hair pulled back in a ponytail. I vaguely remember what they were wearing. I believe Christopher was wearing the same striped shirt from one of the previous dreams, the blue striped shirt.

The boys were in space, surrounded by stars, galaxies, and planets. There also appeared to be small televisions and toys floating around them in a 360-degree circle in space. This dream was one of my last dreams of Christopher.

The Seventh Supernatural Prophetic Dream

*<.>-

In this dream, it was as if Christopher, my son, was watching Mr. N. and my life on a big-screen television. He could see us, and he wanted us to see him too. He watched as we swam in deep waters. There appeared to be yachts or boats in the water that we were swimming in! And he was above us, watching us as we swam. But he wanted us to see him too! I could see him, but Mr. N. could not. So, I kept trying to do things that would help Mr. N. see him, but I'm not sure if Mr. N. ever saw him. And somehow, Mr. N. and I ended up sitting in front of a television where we watched several pictures of the little baby boy pop up on the screen, and sometimes, he took on forms of other children. We saw scenes with a boy hugging his mother. It was as if we were at the movies, watching him in his world. This was the literal dream I had in 2013. Can I explain it? No.

Chapter 8

Connecting the Seventh Dream to Real Life at the Gym

Remember this part of the seventh dream: we sat in front of the television, watching several pictures of our son popping up on the screen, and sometimes, he took on forms of other children.

My Real-Life Experience at the Gym

I had a supernatural moment while at my Zumba dance class at the gym 24 Hour Fitness in 2013. This was an actual physical occurrence at the gym, not a dream.

Since having the dreams and revelations, I have always visualized my son's face flying around me, especially while I danced during Zumba classes. I could see his happy face (literal happy-face images) all around me on the floor, marks on the floor that formed happy faces. And one night, while dancing, I spoke these words out loud, audibly, "Christopher, I love you, Son. I love you, Son; can I fly with you?"

I continued dancing and secretly chanting my same usual chant to him (the words I spoke in the above paragraph), and when I turned while completing a twirl spin, I happened to glance outside the dance room through the big glass window. And standing there, looking in at the dance room, was a woman who just happened to stop in the gym to inquire about membership, and she was holding a little boy, approximately age two or three, in her arms. He was wearing a red shirt and looked exactly like my son in the dream: his hair was reddish-brown or golden and curly; his skin—caramel and face—round. And when I looked at him, he looked at me. I smiled and waved at him. I felt my son's spirit by way of the Holy Spirit was giving me a sign that my son was there with me. Always look for subtle signs.

God is Everything

Finding an Artist to Draw His Face

I got down on my knees and prayed, "God, please help me never to forget his face. I will never forget him or his face."

I could barely utter the above prayer because of the endless flow of tears streaming down my face. I felt so guilty for what I had done and for not giving my son the chance he so desperately deserved. The chance to live. The next step in fulfilling a much-needed promise I made to God and myself was to begin my mission of finding a local artist to recreate the child I had dreamed of so many times. The way I began the task was by thinking about his face and the dreams deeply to ensure accuracy. Secondly, I began reflecting on all the artists I had encountered while shopping or walking on the promenade in Venice or Santa Monica, California. I planned it out in my mind perfectly. I would go to the Santa Monica Pier and find a street artist to recreate the picture of the little boy in my dreams.

Of course, I didn't want to make the journey to the promenade right away because I was a bit nervous about walking up to a complete stranger on the Santa Monica promenade and trying to explain the child's face to him or her. Nevertheless, I knew I had to do it. I contemplated how I would describe him (the little boy in heaven) and how I would explain to the proposed artist who he was and why I didn't have a physical picture that could be replicated. And what happened next was so unbelievable it literally almost took my breath.

The Supernatural Card Sent to Me by Yeshua, God, the Holy Spirit

</\>

The original card was literally sent to me by a priest of the Sacred Heart.

So, it was a normal day for me, nothing out of the ordinary. I went about my apartment, cleaning, as usual. But for whatever reason, I suddenly became disgusted with what felt like overwhelming dirt and filth building up in the room where my office was located. So, I started cleaning and scrubbing it in an effort to remove all the dirt from the room. Mentally, I believe the room and dirt were more of a metaphor for myself. I simply wanted to scrub and remove all the filth and dirt that I felt on or about myself. And I promise you I was on the floor on my hands and knees, crawling around the room, picking things up, and scrubbing dirt off everything.

I guess in exhaustion and an ongoing sadness that simply would not go away, I stopped and paused while breathing deeply. I needed to rest for a minute. I remained on my knees with my body slumped over, leaning forward, crunched in a yogalike child's pose, with my face buried in my arms. I could feel tears in my eyes. I remained in this position for several minutes. And suddenly, for whatever reason, when I began feeling mentally stronger, I lifted my head slightly off the floor and turned to look at the desk sitting to my right. Mind you: this desk was filled with all my old unused Christmas cards, holiday cards, and cards that had been sent to me by several religious organizations to whom I might have given monetary donations. There were also several other pieces of junk that I simply hadn't discarded yet.

And suddenly, like a dove out of heaven, there he was. My mind raced, *It is him; it is him; it is him.* I sat there looking in utter disbelief. How could this be? How could this be happening? I grabbed the card that was staring right at me. I stood up and started running around my house, screaming, crying, and yelling, "Jesus!" for several minutes. I began crying inconsolably as I thought, *Thank God no one is home with me*. My mouth dropped open, my eyes bucked wide, and my heart started racing fast. You would have thought I had just seen a ghost. I literally was having difficulty breathing because I was frozen.

I couldn't believe what my eyes were seeing. *It's impossible*, I thought with my carnal mind, *I can't believe it*. There he was, staring back at me. It was him, the little boy I met in heaven, my son. The exact same child I had met in heaven. I continued screaming and jumping with joy. It was him; whoa, it was really him, the same exact child from the dream. I kept screaming and throwing my hands in the air; I was in complete awe and amazement. There sat in front of me a card of the child I met in heaven—in big, bold color. Jesus heard me. He heard my prayers; He heard my heart; He heard my cries never to forget the face of the beautiful, bright-eyed little boy I met in heaven in my dreams.

I know this is very, very hard for you to believe, as hard as it was for me as well. So, I have tried to make it a little easier for you because seeing is believing. I've attached the photo that was on the front cover of the card that I found on that beautiful, wonderful, supernatural, and

141

miraculous day while crawling on my hands and knees, scrubbing dirt. See the card below.

Best Wishes for Back to School

Back Cover of the Card

Heaven is Real!

Please believe me when I say that heaven is real. I promise you the words I have spoken in this book are true and were sent to me from God, Yeshua, and the Holy Spirit.

Now, I know that some of you might ask: How am I so certain that all of this was from God? And I would answer: because the whole experience was so beautiful, immaculate, and supernatural that it went well above anything my simple mind could ever imagine, especially with my then-typical lifestyle that I would simply describe as selfish, stoic, and evil. But that doesn't mean that I did not think that I was not a good person, oh, quite the contrary. I thought I was perfectly fine. I thought I was a good person because I generally tried to treat people nice, I went to church sometimes, and I believed in God and His Son Yeshua. But I was wrong.

Honestly, I now know without a shadow of a doubt that every word in this card was God's word and supernatural message to me. Every word would soon reveal God's purpose for my life and my supernatural assignment. After all the dreams and supernatural experiences, my heart made of stone was changed forever. Jesus had placed in me a new heart, a new spirit, a new mind, and a saved soul. My life and my attitude to life would never be the same again. I now had a passion for children and Christ that I had never had before. It had now become my mission to reveal God's truth to the world, the truth that He had revealed to me. And my heart hoped that I might be able to save some lives and souls. I was blind, but now I could see.

Inside the Card. Page One

Page number one inside the card reads as follows: "Let the children come to me, for to such belongs the kingdom of God" (Matthew 19:14 and Mark 10:14, paraphrased).

Inside the Card. Page Two

May Yeshua our Lord,
be with you every day

May Yeshua keep you safe from all harm
and treasure you in His Heart
throughout this school year.

The back cover of the card reads as follows, "I will give you a new heart and put a new spirit within you" (Ezekiel 36:26, NKJV).

CHAPTER 9

HEAVEN IS REAL, I ASSURE YOU!

I cannot explain many things that I revealed in this book or how they came to happen or why they happened, but this I know for sure—they happened. The card was sent to me during the time that my spirit and my soul longed for him, my son in heaven. The boy on the card in Jesus's arms is the same boy I dreamed of in the seven dreams. The match was exact. It was not a close resemblance; it was him, exactly as I saw him in the dreams. How do I explain this? There is only one answer: God.

Frankly, as I continued on my journey of discovery, I came to one firm conclusion: man will never fully be able to explain God, Jesus, or the supernatural. "Supernatural" means beyond what the human carnal mind can understand, even when we try. Science, in my opinion, only points us in a direction and attempts to shed light on the great universe inside of us and the one we live in, but there are so many things in our universe that science cannot explain.

Based on what I know of Einstein, he wasn't always a believer in God, but his studies of light, relativity, and $E = Mc^2$ made him a believer. God was in him and his brain, which attempted to point humanity toward the movement of God. Ironically, the very first movie sent to me by way of the supernatural was the documentary on Einstein.

God, our Lord Jesus, and the Holy Spirit are immaculate in every way. One thing I learned through my journey and metamorphosis into developing a new spirit and a new heart is Jesus can and will communicate with us in numerous ways and by using various forms of communication. Some of the ways that have been revealed to me include the Holy Spirit, angels, dreams, visions, wonders, light, objects, pictures, garbage, dust, glitter flakes, balloons, hair, and the list goes on because God is infinite.

Jesus said, "I will send the Holy Spirit to comfort you" (John 14:16, paraphrased).

I have also learned to look for the subliminal messages from God, messages that are often so subtle and occur so quickly that we often miss them. Remember: Jesus often spoke in parables. That said, I would like to highlight the hidden messages in the card that was sent to me, besides the obvious meaning of the card.

Listen:

Prophetic Messages Hidden in the Supernatural Card

Page one of the card said, "Best wishes for being back to school."

The hidden supernatural message was that Jesus would be opening my eyes to the truth of God's will and God's Word. I would be learning something new, hence going back to school to receive new teaching from God. I would be learning the truth and unlearning the lie that we have all been told: that abortion is perfectly fine and that the unformed cells are not a human being because there is no physical body formed as of yet.

What is the purpose of going back to school? The end of something old and the start of something new.

Page two of the card read, "May Jesus, our Lord, be with you every day. May He keep you safe from all harm and treasure you in His heart throughout this school year."

Hidden message: Jesus will see me through the journey. He will protect me from Satan, the evil one, and his demons. God will not let them stop me from achieving His will.

"And treasure you in His heart" was also written on the card.

Jesus revealed to me that he knows my heart and the inner longings of my mind, spirit, and soul. See, I lived my entire life never feeling treasured by anyone. Like *really* treasured. And I remember a supernatural experience I had while I was a guest at Ritz-Carlton shortly after my mother died in 2013. While sitting on my bed, watching television, I saw Ritz-Carlton advertisements scrolling across the television screen. It was the most beautiful advertisement that I had ever seen in my life. Wonderful music was playing in the background as the gorgeous scenic views of the various Ritz-Carlton locations were being displayed. With each scene, there were words and phrases, and in one of the scenes, the words "Let us treasure you" scrolled across the screen. Those words evoked such pain in my heart I began sobbing and crying because I had never felt treasured by anyone in my life.

Jesus's message is: He is all I (you) need, and because He treasures me (you), I (we) no longer need to seek to be treasured by people or princes in the world.

"Let the children come to me, for to such belongs the kingdom of God" (Matthew 19:14 and Mark 10:14, paraphrased).

The message here simply means that every child who dies, either through natural causes, sickness, accident, or murder (abortion), is with God in heaven.

God, What Is My Son's Name?

After the true meaning of the dreams came to light and my eyes were opened to the truth, I started to think what his name might have been if he had been born. What would I name him? Within seconds, I knew I would not have made him a junior. I would have named him Kristopher (with

148

a *K*). And I thought that was it. But it wasn't. Suddenly, I heard a voice say, "Christopher with a *C*." I heard this a few times. Each time I thought of his name that day, I heard the voice say, "Christopher with a *C*."

After all the beautiful, miraculous dreams, visions, sightings, and wonders that had descended upon my life, I thought, *Okay, maybe God's mission has been accomplished. Maybe I saw the last of the dreams now that my son's identity and name have been revealed to me?* I wondered if the dreams would stop. I certainly hoped not; I wanted to see him again and again, hold him in my arms, and let him know just how much I really, really loved him. I wanted him to know I cared and would search for him for the rest of my life—in my dreams, through signs, through visions, through wonderings—wherever I had to go to find him, I would go there. Whatever I had to do, I would do that. I would not fail him again. This was the least I could do after all I had done to him.

My guilt was tremendous, even though I knew this was not the intention of God in revealing my son to me, but guilt is a natural byproduct of sin. I had ended a life that was intended to be lived. Christopher came as love, as *agape* love, a love that only Jesus can give. The love that says, "Even though you didn't need me, somehow, I needed you, and I love you because all I know is love."

Even if it required that I search a trash bin or walk around, looking for signs on the ground, in the trees, in the sky, through Christmas lights, balloons, glitter spots on the floor, hearts magically appearing in my discarded hair, or images made from dirt and debris, it didn't matter. Whatever I had to do to find a hint of my son's presence with me, I would do for the rest of my natural life until he and I could meet again in heaven.

But God showed me something. No matter how or where I looked, I didn't have to struggle to find Him. When it was time, God would reveal Himself to me, in one form or another.

A Spontaneous Supernatural Miracle Moment

On my gosh! While typing the above paragraph, the following words appeared on my television screen by way of an advertisement: "Amazing Grace," with Aretha Franklin's photo next to it. See, this is what I mean by unexpected occurrences happening that I cannot explain, supernatural wonders. Food for thought: Does that mean that all things that happen are according to God's divine plan?

Don't Forget the Story of the Donkey in the Bible

Don't forget the biblical story where God used a donkey and a burning bush to deliver a message. Remember: the donkey talked to Balaam. Suddenly, God gave the donkey speech: "What have I done to you that you beat me these three times?" the donkey asked Balaam (Numbers 22:28, paraphrased).

Through the burning bush, God talked to Moses. That said, there are no limits to what, how, or who God can use to communicate His message.

However, the answer is no: the dreams did not stop. They continued, and not only did they continue, but they also continued to reveal several treasures from heaven, including a trip to a hell-like place. I personally don't believe one can go to hell and return from it. However, I do believe God took me to a place, hell's gate, or a prophetic point in time of something that will take place in the future. I truly can't explain what it was, but I can tell you it was scary and it was bad.

The Eighth Supernatural Prophetic Dream

He wanted to know my name.

This was a lucid dream, where I was not fully asleep, not like in REM sleep, a deep seventh-stage dream. I was working at my computer and just slightly dosed off.

While dosing, I felt drifting into another world where I could hear an audible conversation between a little boy and a woman. The woman's voice was a breathy, airy one, like that of Marilyn Monroe but far more beautiful, deep, and holy. Imagine an airy, breathy contralto that carried the beauty of a soft wind like a harp sound, blowing warmth across your face. That said, here is what happened next:

I heard a little boy's voice say, "La Treeeee na," as though he was trying to understand the phonetic pronunciation of my true name. And I heard the woman's voice respond, "La Treeeee na."

And then I awoke. I was visibly shaken as I lifted my head and looked at my computer. I knew the voice belonged to the little boy I had met in haven. I knew it without any doubt. The women's voice was so powerful I wanted to know who she was as well. I imagined she was a guardian angel watching over the children. But I didn't give much thought to who she was, well, at least not as much thought as I gave to imagining the conversation they (Christopher and the woman) were having. Why was he pronouncing my original name, one before my name changed? Oh, I figured it out.

The woman was teaching him to say my name, and he was learning my name and how to pronounce it correctly. I imagined that he was curious about my name, now that he knew who I was and had had the opportunity to meet me. It was my belief that he asked the woman, "What is her name?" and the woman responded with my true name. As I sat there thinking, tears welled up in my eyes, and I began to weep uncontrollably. I couldn't stop asking myself how I could be so cruel, so cruel. But I knew the answer wasn't that I was innately evil, no, not at all. The answer was that

I was ignorant of the truth. I simply didn't understand life, God, and the Holy Spirit. I was the blind being led to the slaughter (hell) by the blind like those in the Bible verse that says, "They are blind leaders of the blind. And if the blind leads the blind, both will fall into a ditch" (Matthew 15:14, NKJV).

I sat on my bed, completely astonished, completely breath taken. How did I know this lucid dream was real and from heaven? Because if I had had my choice in the matter, I would have never ever said the name I heard the woman (angel) say. Never. Thus, I realized that this was a true incarnation of God because I had no control over the dream or how the message would be delivered to my son. Nor would I have ever included it in this book if it were not absolutely necessary and a truth from God. But because it was from God and part of my supernatural experience, I had no choice but to include it in this book; otherwise, I would be hiding a truth God revealed. This lucid dream further solidified that God's thoughts are different from ours. What we might see as right (i.e., name change), God might see as wrong.

I further identified this lucid dream as being from God because God cannot lie, and the truth is, my birth name is my true name; thus, if the dream were not from God, my chosen name (Taylor Coco) would have been given to my son rather than my birth name. Obviously, God approved of my birth name, even when I didn't.

Correlations of the Eighth Lucid Dream with the Bible

When the Holy Spirit, the angel of God, descended from heaven to speak to Saul, who later became Paul, the voice from heaven spoke to Saul:

> And he fell to the earth, and heard a voice saying unto him, Saul, Saul, why persecutest thou me? [...] And the men who journeyed with him [Saul] stood speechless, hearing a voice, but seeing no man.

> **Acts 9:4, 7**

CHAPTER 10

A GOD MOMENT

A Supernatural Sign That God Hears Our
Questions and Our Thoughts

Fast-forward to the moment I sat typing this dream: I believe I had a miraculous experience where the Holy Spirit revealed to me the identity of the woman in this dream. While typing the dream (March 17, 2019), I began coughing terribly because I was just getting over a terrible head cold. As I reached for a piece of Kleenex, which I kept in a drawer sitting to the right of my bed, I accidentally pulled out the whole box and noticed it was almost empty. *Oh no*, I thought, *this is not enough tissue*. Suddenly, Mr. N. walked into the room, and I called out to him, "Perfect timing! Can you get me a new box of Kleenex?" Mr. N. returned with the box, and I reached into the drawer to pull out the old Kleenex box, and while I was doing so, a small card, which was hidden behind the box, fell out. The card was from the Sisters of St. Francis of Assisi. On the card was the story of the miracle of Lourdes, with a picture of

Mary, the mother of Jesus, on the front cover of the card.

This supernatural moment literally occurred as I was typing the above paragraph about the lucid dream of the woman's voice speaking to the little boy.

The picture below of the Blessed Virgin Mother Mary fell out of my drawer (where it had been stored behind a book for some time without being touched). I cannot explain it. I will not even try to.

O Mother
of the sick,
look with mercy
on me and
comfort me
in my time
of trouble.

The card described a supernatural occurrence that took place in 1858 at a grotto in a little village in southwest France. Mary appeared eighteen times to a young woman named Bernadette Soubirous, announcing, "I am the immaculate conception." This is known as the miracle of Lourdes. This card fell out of a spot where I had originally placed it some time ago as I typed the passage about the lucid dream.

As I continued typing, it suddenly came to me: after the lucid dream, for many years, I wondered about the voice of the woman speaking to Christopher in the dream. I often wondered who she was. Who could she be? I gathered from her protective voice that she was some sort of guide or protector of the children. After this supernatural moment, I truly came to believe that the voice of the mystery woman in the dream was that of the Blessed Virgin Mother Mary, the mother of Jesus Christ, our Lord and Savior.

God is not limited in how He can reveal hidden truths to us. I beseech you to keep your eyes and ears open to the supernatural world of hidden gems: mysteries, signs, and wonders.

The Ninth Dream

Christopher's Visitation

This dream was a bit scary and very different from all the other dreams. The ninth dream was a paralyzed sleep, where I could feel a presence in my room, but I could not awake myself. And the presence literally touched me. This time something or someone came to me in the spiritual realm. I believe it was him, my son Christopher. I know, I know: it sounds unfathomable. Trust me: I felt the same way when I awoke. However, keep in mind: paralyzed dreams are not unheard of. Many people have reported experiencing paralysis during lucid and REM sleep.

Paralyzed Sleep

Have you ever fallen asleep and, somewhere in the middle of the night, began to feel paralyzed from head to toe, and somehow you fell into a lucid sleep, where you really were not asleep but just sleepy enough to feel as though you were awake but dreaming? Okay, so that is what happened that night. I fell asleep as usual, never expecting anything out of the ordinary to happen.

Suddenly, while sleeping, in the dead of night, my entire body became paralyzed, and I knew there was a presence in the room with me, but I could not open my eyes and could not move. I continued to lay there helplessly, frozen and frightened, very frightened. Although this was not my first experience with paralyzed sleep dreams, it was still extremely difficult and frightening. As the sleep paralysis continued, I suddenly felt something crawling up my legs from my toes. In that moment, I didn't know what it was—a thing, a person, or an object—slowly moving or crawling up my legs. To put it politely: I was horrified.

As the crawling continued up my legs, it or he reached the area of my body where my ovaries are located. Within seconds, I began to feel pressure on my right ovary. It felt as though something was sitting or lying there on my right ovary for at least one minute. It didn't hurt, but I was desperately trying to move or scream because I was scared. My attempts to move or scream were useless: I could do neither. After what felt like three to five minutes, my body was released, and the presence was gone. I immediately felt relieved.

Quite remarkably, I didn't awake after the experience; I just drifted back off to sleep. However, the fear was significant enough for me to remember the feeling and the dream the next morning. My initial thoughts were, *Why had it come, and what was it?* At the time, I had no idea, but the one thing I was sure of was that I didn't want it to happen again. I didn't like the feeling of being paralyzed while I slept. I later came to believe that it was my son's spirit coming down from heaven to visit me. Nothing like this has ever happened since, and for that, I am grateful. As a human being, I am still very uneasy with the presence of supernatural forces that cause me to experience paralysis while I sleep.

The Fourth Supernatural Prophetic Movie

Mars Needs Moms

{...}

This movie came to me after the paralyzed sleep. By habit, I never sleep with the television off. At approximately 3:30 a.m., I was awoken by the television. The noise level of the movie had awakened me. When I opened my eyes, there was a cartoon movie playing. Even as I sit here typing, I do not know how I managed to stay awake to watch the whole movie, but after awakening from my sleep, my eyes were pierced to it. When the movie ended, I cried, and I knew that it was Christopher speaking to me through a prophetic movie. I knew it was God; I knew it was Jesus, and I knew it was the Holy Spirit delivering a message to me from God and my son. The essence of the movie was as follows:

The main character in the movie was a young *red-haired* boy who had lost his mom to aliens. The aliens visited his home one night, stole his mother from the house, and took her to Mars. However, as the aliens were taking off to go back home to Mars in their spaceship, the little boy managed to attach himself to the outer part of the spaceship and snuck on board.

The general theme was he wanted to find and save his mother from the aliens. So, he left the earth and went to space (the second heaven) in search of his mother.

- Hence, this is another movie that I just happened to awake to or stumble upon, where there was a boy with red hair, looking for his mother or trying to save his mother.

- In like manner, the dreams of my son Christopher (Chris–to–[p]her: "Christ to her") were sent to me to help save me and to show me that I have a son who loves me and wants to be with me in heaven.

The title *Mars Needs Moms* is so striking and unmistakably correlated with the theme of all my dreams. Christopher needed me, even when I didn't need him.

Heaven needs moms too.

The Fifth Supernatural Prophetic Movie

Holes

(*-*)

This movie is ironically another movie about a child who was separated from his mother by no choice of his own. He was a castaway who had been sent away to prison and was being raised by a foster family. He was unhappily apart from his mother and had pretty much become a mute until he found a friend he could trust. The movie ended with him and his biological mother being reunited happily ever after.

The Sixth Supernatural Prophetic Movie

Happy Thank You More Please

7

The sixth movie is a 2010 romantic comedy-drama film.

This movie is about the struggles that several pairs, trying to find their way, face. The film focuses on a writer and a foster child named Rasheen, who met each other when Rasheen was abandoned by his mother and father on a subway.

This movie, like all the others, came on in a very incidental fashion. So, honestly, I barely paid attention to it. After a few minutes of watching, I noticed a familiar little boy with a striking resemblance to all the other little boys in the previous movies, who I happened to stumble upon, either while awake or while sleeping. Most importantly, each of the little boys in all the supernaturally sent movies resembled *the* little boy (my son Christopher wearing the red onesie) in all my dreams. Secondly, this movie, like all the others, was about a little boy who had been abandoned by his mother and father.

Rasheen was a foster child looking for a home and a friendly family to take him in and love him.

See below the list of the striking similarities of all the movies that I happened to awake to, usually in the middle of the night and always around 3:00 a.m. or 3:30 a.m., with the exception of the one seen at the movies, but even that one was not chosen by me.

‘‘‘ *
—

The major theme of all the movies was unveiled through a male child with red hair, desperately seeking his mom. Each child was either orphaned or abandoned, tragically or comically separated from his mother. Each appeared sad because of being separated from his mother.

Because of the similarity of the theme in all of the movies and the fact that I did not choose any of these movies, but they were chosen for me, I knew they were supernatural and sent by God (Yahweh) through the Holy Spirit. These movies were similar to the dreams and typically involved the boy looking for and finding his mother.

Correlation with the Little Baby Boy in My Dreams

My heavenly son, Christopher: (1) had red curly hair; (2) somehow came or was sent back to the earth to find and help save me (his mother), and (3) was an orphan in heaven who had been abandoned by his mother (me).

Ask yourselves: What are the odds of me happening upon all the movies listed above with the same running theme? And in each movie, all of the little boys had the same hair color as the little boy in my dreams. And the little boy in the picture has the same hair color as all of the little boys in the movies. Sounds a bit mysterious, huh? Yes, that's what I said as well.

If there is one thing I have learned from the Bible, it is that Jesus often spoke in parables, and God can use any form of communication to speak to humans: "I will not leave you as orphans; I will come to you," said Yeshua in John 14:18 (ESV).

There Was a Total of Ten Movies

The first movie, a documentary, *Einstein*: understanding the universe, the physical movement from flesh to energy (spirit), then from matter content (flesh) back to energy (spirit), God. $E = Mc^2$.

In the second movie, *Meet Joe Black*, death was allowed to return to the earth for a short time and dwell among humans and a particular family.

The connection to my story: the supernatural visitations from my son, who died but was allowed to return to the earth for a short time to see and visit his earthly mother.

The third movie documentary, *Nature*: a leopard cub experienced a horrific experience with a baboon and was thought to have died after the baboon attacked it. But it miraculously survived the attack and, hours later, returned to its mother.

The connection to my story: though my son died a physical death, he did not die ultimately because his spirit, his soul, lives in heaven. The supernatural visitations and a return to his mother (in the spirit) on the earth is what I truly believe happened in my case.

In the fourth movie, *Mars Needs Moms*, a boy leaves the earth to go to Mars to find and save his mother from aliens.

In the fifth movie, *Holes*, an orphaned little boy, thought to be abandoned by his mother, found and reconnected with his mother.

In the sixth movie, *Happy Thank You More Please*, a foster child, an orphaned little boy, was saved by a man who helped guide him to a family that would love and raise him. He became his friend by taking him in and helping him find a home.

The seventh movie, a documentary, was *I Survived... Beyond and Back* (April 22, 2012).

And then there were supernatural movies involving unseen spirits.

The eighth movie, *Casper*, came on sometime around 3:00 a.m. in the morning while I slept on my birthday, December 10, in the year 2012. The theme of this supernatural movie was slightly different from the others. In the case of *Casper*, a young boy had died prematurely but was alive in the spirit world and continued to dwell on the earth.

His dwelling on the earth as a spirit is what I believe is the connection to my son and supernatural visitations.

In the ninth movie, *Dark Shadows*, a young boy longed for his mother, who had died a short time earlier. His father was largely disinterested in him or his existence. However, he still had a connection to his deceased mother through the spirit world. In the case of this movie, the mother was the spirit; however, this movie, like all the other supernatural movies that had been sent to me, had a common theme. A young boy longed to have and be with his mother.

Regarding the Supernatural Prophetic
Movie Dark Shadows

All the other movies share the theme of a child (little boy) being separated from his mother. In the case of the movie *Dark Shadows*, it was not the little boy who died, but it was his mother who died. However, he still went about the house where he lived, searching for her and feeling her spirit. He had a special connection to his mother's spirit, which he could see and speak to. In the case of this movie, I believed the supernatural message to be (in like manner with all the other movies) a boy longing for his mother so much so that he could cross over into her world (the spirit world).

A Supernatural Day at the Movies
(a Real-Life Experience, Not a Dream)

The thing to note is I had never planned to see this movie, nor did I have any desire to. This movie was the only choice I had because of the mistake the movie theater made when selling tickets for the movie I originally wanted to see. The movie theater was oversold for the day, and the only seats left were for the movie *Dark Shadows*. There were exactly five seats together in the last row in the movie. After we had gotten over our disappointment, we found our row and seats and took our spots. There was one interesting thing I noticed after we all took our seats: there were four of us, but there were five seats available. The fifth seat, one which remained open, was the seat located on my right. And after watching the movie and realizing what it was about, I knew the open seat and the change in movies was no accident.

Suppose the correlation with all the other movies and the accidental tickets for a movie I never planned to see doesn't seem odd enough. How about the Carpenters who are in this movie performing and singing another one of their songs? Irony or coincidence?

Karen Carpenter's Voice and Songs
Revealing God's Voice, Revealing God's Love

I believe the message of the Holy Spirit in the case of Karen Carpenter (being that she was presented to me twice: in a song and in a movie) is: (1), she had a very comforting voice that wooed millions of people, and (2), her songs were usually comforting, fun, and uplifting. Such is the intended message indicating that the children in heaven are being comforted by a comforter who sings songs and melodies that are sweet and beautiful to their ears.

First was the supernatural song, "Bless the Beasts and the Children," the Carpenters' song sent to me by the Holy Spirit, and then I accidentally ended up at the theater in a movie for which I had not purchased tickets.

The Tenth Supernatural Prophetic Documentary Movie

Antoni Gaudi

*0-I-0

The tenth movie was a documentary about Antoni Gaudi, a famous architect who was building a cathedral for God called La Sagrada Familia, a basilica in Barcelona, Spain. In 1883, he was commissioned to build a cathedral, the Basilica de la Sagrada Familia, which became known as his main work. Gaudi devoted the remainder of his life to the construction of this project. He referred to the cathedral as the house of God. Antoni died in a horrible accident before the completion of the project. La Sagrada Familia is a large unfinished Roman Catholic minor basilica in the Eixample district of Barcelona.

Interestingly, based on what I saw in the documentary, the cathedral may still not be complete. Some of the project's greatest challenges remain unfinished, including the construction of ten spires, each symbolizing an important biblical figure in the New Testament. The anticipated completion date is 2026, the centenary of Gaudi's death.

Gaudi's death is very eerily similar to the death of our Lord and Savior Jesus (Yeshua) and the deaths of aborted children. Here are a few interesting facts:

When Gaudi was killed, he was walking to or from the cathedral he was building. He was walking in the streets

168

and had the look of a commoner, not of a person of great esteem or that of a great architect. He was run over by the driver of a street tram who did not see him when he stepped out into the road. It was a very sad, unfortunate, and unpredictable death. Even when the driver of the tram finally realized that he had run over a human being, he initially thought it was a homeless vagrant. The driver of the tram, the one who took Gaudi's life, had no idea that the man he had accidentally run over and killed was one of the greatest and most brilliant architects to ever live. An architect for Christ.

This was because Gaudi was dressed very normally, like a person who would appear poor. And at the time that he was run over, no one else walking in the streets recognized or knew that it was him. What I found interesting when I stumbled upon the Gaudi story is how he died. He looked like someone of no importance. No one was even paying any attention to him as he walked the streets that day. His brilliance and importance could not be seen by onlookers (with the naked eye) because he presented himself with no esteem, importance, or wealth. He was not gaudy or vainglorious in appearance on this day at all. And when he died, his body was crushed by the tram. So, in essence, in many ways, Gaudi's death shares some striking similarities to the deaths of aborted children and Jesus.

Aborted children are not seen by the naked eye or by onlookers as actually being a noteworthy life. They are not deemed as important or as worthy of life because, in essence, they are nobody. And when they die, they are crushed to death by the suction devices, medical tools used to remove them from their mother's cervix. The doctor who kills them does not even see the life in them when he is suctioning their lives away. But, just as the driver who killed Gaudi, the doctor will one day discover the mistakes of his follies. He will one day realize that the life he took was a very important person to someone, to God.

Also, Jesus, in like manner, was actually a very important person, a very distinguished person, the Son of God, who was mistaken for a nobody by the Pharisees and others when they sent Him to the crucifixion. But the importance of who Jesus was could not be seen with the naked eye because He made Himself as if of no esteem; he was not gaudy, vainglorious, and did not want to be crowned or adorned with the title "king" or receive any of the accolades that came with that title. But later, in like fashion, the veils on their eyes were lifted, and the glory of Yeshua, which extends far beyond this earth, was seen and known by all of humanity.

I believe God's hidden message in this documentary is as follows: all alive children, outside or inside the mother's womb, like in Gaudi's case, are very important human beings who are unfortunately mistaken for being no one of any importance or significance. Thus, human babies (human life) in the womb are being crushed to death and thrown away by those who cannot see them or their value at all. I believe this documentary has a deep-hidden mysterious message being unveiled.

In 2013, Gaudi's cathedral was still under construction, and some believe the cathedral to be God's house, which is still under construction. Will God return when the cathedral is complete? I don't know; it's just something to think about as we look around us daily and see the dismal state of the world that we live in.

"And this gospel of the kingdom will be proclaimed throughout the whole world as a testimony to all the nations, and then the end will come" (Matthew 24:14, ESV).

CHAPTER 11

A SUPERNATURAL PROPHETIC CONFIRMATION THAT HEAVEN IS AND MY DREAMS WERE REAL

The seventh movie was a real-life documentary about people who had near-death experiences (NDEs).

I Survived…Beyond and Back

April 22, 2012

Again, while surfing the channels, I stumbled upon a show called *I Survived…Beyond and Back* on the Biography HD channel. Somewhat magically, this documentary popped up on my screen one night while I was watching television.

Honestly, as I started watching the show, I couldn't take my eyes off my television because since I started experiencing all the visions and dreams, my interest in the supernatural was at an all-time high. I had been experiencing several supernatural occurrences, dreams, visions,

sightings, wonders, the finding of heavenly physical artifacts, and seeing physical signs. This documentary came
after all the dreams of my son in heaven. So, of course,
without question, I was interested in a show with the prem-
ise that someone had died and come back from death to tell
the world about their experiences.

Ironically, this was another movie about death or someone returning from death that I just happened to stumble
upon. That said, I truly believe that God, Jesus, and the
Holy Spirit led me to this documentary (like all the others
as well).

As I sat watching and listening to all the recounts of
near-death experiences (NDE) by the people being interviewed, I almost fell to the floor, with my mouth hanging
open and eyes swelling with tears. And then came the story
of Kerry. I could not believe my ears. I could not believe
what I heard Kerry describe. How could it be that he and I
(two people who have never met) visited the same place in
heaven? What he described in his NDE is so similar to the
place I visited in my dreams that I truly believe we both
went to the same place in heaven, except in his NDE, he
was allowed to see the outside of the home as well as the
inside. However, the home that I was in did not appear to
have the roof torn off, nor did it appear dilapidated. It was
quite the opposite: cozy, warm, breezy, and comfortable.

Kerry

Bagdad, Kentucky

October 2008

I Survived...Beyond and Back, Biography Channel, aired
on April 22, 2012

Kerry's story is so crazy I would not have believed it
had I not seen and heard it for myself. My rendition of the
interview is a paraphrase of the actual interview.

Kerry and his friend were motorcycle racing. Kerry
was not wearing a helmet. He was going 110 miles per
hour and suddenly turned a corner, and there was a truck
traveling on the opposite side of the road, heading straight
toward him. Kerry was traveling too fast to stop in time,
and the truck hit him head-on.

At the scene of the accident, Kerry lost six pints of
blood, and one of his legs was ripped off his body. In the
documentary, Kerry's friend described how Kerry flew into
the air, landed on the back of his head, and slid off the road
into a ditch. Kerry indicated that his lungs had shut down
and that he wasn't breathing. He said he had no blood left
in him and that there was no way he could have still been
alive at the crash scene. On impact, he completely blacked
out and flatlined. Kerry's injuries were stage four critical,
and his friend thought he was dead.

It was so bad Kerry had to be airlifted to the nearest
medical hospital. During the moments that he had flatlined
(technically dead), he experienced the following, as de-

scribed in his own words:

Kerry speaks about his near-death experience (NDE) and fatal motorcycle accident:

"The first memory I have is I was in this place, a small brick house. I felt a presence of protection around me. Like I was just being protected. I had a warm feeling all over, and I never felt more secure in my life than I did then. Then within a split second, I was in a room; it was a large room; it was almost like an abandoned house. The roof had been blown in, and the top was hanging down. There was a man and a woman, a young couple. There were fifteen or twenty little kids running around, playing. For some reason, I had a feeling that they were in there for some kind of care, for some kind of treatment, almost just like daycare.

"These people were watching over these children very well and making sure they were taken care of. All these little kids were having fun. They were shaking my hand and running around laughing.

"And then, all of a sudden, I'm not there anymore. I am at another building. It looked like a truck stop or something. There were several tables and chairs like a diner would have in it. But as soon as I entered and sat down, this lady said, 'Does anyone know how to drive a truck? I need this truck moved.' I looked outside, and I saw a kind of red-goldish Peterbilt truck, an eighteen-wheeler sitting out in front of this building. I have a class A CDL license, so I went outside, got in this truck, and moved it just to the side of the building.

"That's all I remember of that place. It never did occur to me that I was dead or dying at the time. I was feeling no pain. It was confusing to me, and I wondered, 'What's going on here?' It wasn't a dream; I know for sure. Then, I was hovering over at a low altitude. I could see myself and a metal object disconnecting my body from my internal organs. I was in no pain; I had no worries. Immediately, I was about a hundred feet up in the air, looking down at this twenty-twenty-yard patch of dirt, and it had a bulldozer sitting beside it. There was nobody working, and there was water on the other side of the place where the bulldozer was sitting. It was as clear and vivid as we are sitting here today. I was floating above it, and that's the last I remember of that scene. The next thing I remember is I was waking up."

The man in the above story is real, and his near-death experience is a true story. One thing that solidified that the accident he described had actually happened was that when he stood up at the end of the interview, he was missing a full leg. But I promise you, if you read and look closely at his depiction of his heavenly experience during his near-death experience, you will see that his depiction of this place in heaven was almost identical to the place I described in my first dream of Christopher, my son in heaven. Keep in mind: Kerry and I have never ever met.

My first dream of Christopher, where I was taken to

heaven, occurred in 2012, prior to my viewing of the show that Kerry was in.

My Dreams Compared to Kerry's Real-Life Traumatic Story, Near-Death Experience, and Account of His Trip to Heaven

My dream:

In my first dream of heaven, I was in a house (I could not tell the size of the house).

Kerry:

When Kerry died, he immediately found himself in a small brick house.

My dream:

I was in a house filled with children laughing and playing. I could not see the children, but I could hear them.

Kerry:

While Kerry was in the house, not only could he hear the children laughing, he could also see them, and they came up to him and touched him and grabbed his hand to shake it.

My dream:

I sat on a large, very comfortable couch, and a child sat next to me on my left side. The child was wearing a red-and-white onesie.

Kerry:

While Kerry was speaking on television during the interview, he was wearing a red-and-white shirt.

My dream:

In my second dream of heaven, I saw a hand that reached in and handed me a bowl to feed Christopher. I also heard the voice of a woman pronounce my name in one of the first seven dreams.

Kerry:

While Kerry was in the house, not only did he see the children laughing and playing, but he also saw a female and a male caretaker for the children. This establishes that there was a female in the house he was taken to upon his death.

My dream:

In my first dream of heaven, the little baby boy ran out of the house. I ran after him, trying to keep him from running into the road to save his life. Upon exiting the house, I saw a huge red diesel truck driving down the street, approaching the little baby boy who was running so fast he almost appeared to be flying. Unfortunately, he ran into the street and was hit by the truck, crushed, and killed. I never saw what the house actually looked like on the outside (besides the chain-link fence) because I woke up immediately after the little baby boy was hit by the truck.

Kerry:

Kerry described himself drifting into or flashing into another scene (immediately) where he was outside of the house and ended up inside a diner, where a woman requested for someone to drive a diesel truck, and he volunteered.

The color he described the truck as being was either an exact match to the truck in my dream or very close. But definitely, the style and size of the truck he saw were exactly the same as of the truck I saw. Kerry said that he got into the truck and moved it to the other side of the diner and that was it for that dream. The truck moved from one side of the diner to the other side, almost as if he moved the truck from one side of the road to the other side.

Also note: Kerry was hit head-on by an oncoming truck, which smashed his body and ripped off one of his legs at the hip. It is so eerie that the color of Kerry's shirt during the interview matched the color of the onesie the little baby boy was wearing in my dream.

Finally, Kerry:

Kerry's trip to heaven landed him in one more scene, the last, the final part of his supernatural experience: "Immediately, I am about a hundred feet up in the air, looking down at this twenty-twenty-yard patch of dirt, and it had a bulldozer sitting beside it. There was nobody working, and there was water on the other side of this place where the bulldozer was sitting."

I actually do not have a corresponding dream to this scene. However, I do have my interpretation of the meaning of this scene. Whether it is correct, I am not sure, but I believe I am. Judge for yourselves.

The Angels Are in the Details

The bulldozer sat next to a twenty-twenty patch of dirt: bulldozers are sometimes used to remove dirt when the cemetery workers prepare a grave for someone's burial.

There was nobody working: a bit strange and eerie. But in heaven, there will be no toiling or pain.

There was water on the other side of the place where the bulldozer sat: paradise awaits after the storm passes. Water represents calm, a sense of peace after the terrible events.

Ironic Correlation Number One

The bulldozer sat next to a twenty-twenty patch of dirt. Irony: Kerry's accident might have occurred in 2008; four years later, in 2012, Kerry's interview aired; eight years after Kerry's interview aired came the year of 2020, which will forever be known as the year of great death and devastation to the family (COVID-19).

Ironic Correlation Number Two

The number of children Kerry estimated to be in the home he saw in heaven was fifteen to twenty. Kerry's video aired on April 22, 2012. Exactly eight months later, twenty children were brutally murdered by a madman in what came to be known as the Sandy Hook massacre.

The Ironic Number Eight

The time frame between the occurrence of each of the above incidents is eight years or months. In the Bible, the number eight means a new beginning, meaning a new order or creation, and the "born again" event when he or she is resurrected from the dead into eternal life. According to some, the number eight is considered a symbol of creation and new beginnings. It is a known fact that Jesus resurrected on Nisan 17, but if we take into account that seventeen is composed of numbers one and seven, hence $1 + 7 = 8$. Nisan 17 was actually the eighth day from the day on which Jesus was selected to be sacrificed. Because of this, it can be said that the number eight could be a symbol of sacrifice.

The Irony of the House

Finally, Kerry said, "Then within a split second, I was in a room; it was a large room; it was almost like an abandoned house. The roof had been blown in, and the top was hanging down."

The human body in the Bible is sometimes referred to as a house or a temple that houses the spirit and the soul. Jesus said, "Destroy this temple, and in three days, I will raise it up" (John 2:19).

I believe the torn and broken house symbolically represented the bodies of the children that were torn and ripped apart while here on the earth.

Conversation with My Niece,

My Mother's Granddaughter, Sometime in 2014

Today several incidents happened that made me realize that my mother (in spirit) wanted me to call my sister.

One of the signs was when a butterfly that I had dedicated to my mother fell onto the floor next to a book that I had purchased for my sister. The butterfly fell to the floor for no apparent reason.

So, I decided to call my sister, whom I had not spoken to in quite a while. After one or two rings, Erica, my mother's granddaughter, answered the phone. "Hello, beautiful," I said. She responded, "Hi, Auntie." And the next few words out of her mouth were very interesting, to say the least.

Without any rhyme or reason, she began asking me about my children. She wanted to know where they were and asked if she could speak to them. She was so determined to speak to a person or persons she really didn't even know existed. I mean, I had never told her that I had children, and she had never asked about them before. However, as I sat there in silence for a couple of minutes, she continued to press me with the same question, I guess, until she got what she wanted: an answer or a chance to speak to my children.

Keep in mind: this was never a conversation that she and I had ever had before. She was only seven years old. Finally, following a little chuckle, I gave in and said, "I have two sons," and began explaining to her who they were and how they were related to her, meaning they were her first cousins. After I finished telling her about my two sons, these were her exact words to me: "Why don't you have three children? Do you want three children?"

I broke down and cried because I knew I had forgotten to tell her about my third child, the one in heaven, Christopher. But somehow, she knew of my third child in heaven; she knew I had a third child. So, I told her his name was Christopher and that he was with Grandma in heaven. Her voice grew louder with excitement, and she replied, "Yes, I have a friend named Christopher in my class; Christopher is my friend." She was so excited to hear the name "Christopher" I could feel her jumping out of her seat through the phone. But when I told her my other son's names, she did not exhibit the same level of excitement.

I couldn't believe it—the truth spoken from the mouth of a seven-year-old child. The biggest question ruminating in my mind was: How did she know? How could she have known of him, my son in heaven? And if that wasn't enough, immediately after hanging up with her, I turned on the television, and there was a famous pastor (J. Duplantis) speaking about aborted children in heaven and telling all mothers that they have children waiting for them in heaven. He was speaking as a guest on a famous religious talk show.

Undeniably, I understood my conversation with my niece and the message from the famous pastor on television immediately following the conversation I had with my niece as a prophetic message from God, Jesus (Yeshua), the Holy Spirit, my mother, and Christopher, my son third son in heaven.

Shortly after watching the religious talk show, I fell asleep with my television on. When I awoke (briefly) in the middle of the night, the following two messages appeared on my screen:

"Meditate within your heart on your bed, and be still" (Psalm 4:4, NKJV).

When I looked up at the television a second time, the message read, "Be still and know that I am God" (Psalm 46:10).

CHAPTER 12

THE SHIMMERING SPARKLE

The Third Child's Story

The Third Child (Top Left Corner of the Picture)

*_ _
_
[^]

DeJesus. A True Story (Not a Dream)

DeJesus's story is a true one, or better said, actual events that took place within the earthly realm. I did not have any dreams of DeJesus; however, his face was one of the four children on the card that was sent to me by the priest of the Sacred Heart.

Like all the other children's stories that I've told you this far, DeJesus's story also fell upon me like a star descending from heaven. Like with all the other supernatural wonders and occurrences, I was not expecting DeJesus's story to be revealed to me. Like with all the others, I was not aware that he (the second little boy in the picture) had a story that would be revealed. However, being that I had started experiencing several strange and miraculous wonders, visions, and dreams, I had a feeling that the entire picture contained majestic hidden supernatural secrets waiting to be revealed. Hence, every child featured on the card had significant meaning. God is omnipotent and more exact than physics. There are no mistakes or coincidences with God.

Before I tell you the story of DeJesus, I want to mention the picture with the four children first. The picture of the four children has remained by my bedside, sitting on a nightstand ever since I received it from the priests in early 2012. The picture created a strong bond between my son Christopher and me, so instinctively, every day, I looked at the picture, longing for his loving spirit to return to me again. Sometimes when I looked at it, I cried out of sheer grief. It wasn't long before I began noticing that the picture had begun to develop a little shimmer, sparkles all over it. I believe the shimmer, the sparkles, might have originated from me kissing the picture and/or holding it next to my heart when I cried.

Being a "girly" girl, I loved shimmery things and lotions with body glitter but never intentionally placed glitter or sparks of glitter on the picture. However, on any given night, I may glance at the picture, and depending on the lighting in the room, a speck of glitter would shine somewhere on the picture. The card almost appeared to speak to me through the glitter. Today I fully understand that the Holy Spirit was sending subtle miraculous messages to me.

For instance, with the other two children (Sparkle Eyes and Christopher), on occasion, a little spark of glitter would appear on the faces, cheeks, or forehead of one of them. But never would the speck of glitter appear on both children at the same time; it was always one or the other. However, a speck of glitter shining on one of the children happened very infrequently and randomly.

Notably, each time a spark of glitter appeared on or next to a particular child, soon thereafter, that particular child's story would be revealed to me by God, Jesus, and the Holy Spirit. And each time, I was literally left speechless, in awe, and completely breath taken.

>*<

On May 7, 2013, at approximately 7:00 (Pacific Standard Time), while looking at my picture, as I often did, I noticed something that I had not noticed for quite some time: a sparkle, a small shimmer on the face of one of the children. I moved closer to the picture to see if I was actually seeing what I thought I was seeing. And yes, I was correct: there was a small spark of glimmer shining bright on the back of the head of the little Latino boy. As I looked at the picture, I pondered, *Why tonight? Why is shimmer, a sparkle shining on the back of his head tonight?* His sparkle was very bright and distinct. It stood out, shining so bright I could not have missed it.

Now, I should be clear: I did not know his name at this moment or prior to this night. His name (DeJesus) would be revealed to me at a later time.

As I stood over the picture, looking at it shimmering, I was in awe, so I instinctively started speaking to the picture (out loud). I actually looked at the picture and asked, "What are you trying to tell me? God, what is the message? What is he trying to tell me?" As I continued looking at the Latino child, speaking to the picture, I said the following words: "I don't know your story yet, but I will wait for God, Jesus, and the Holy Spirit to reveal it to me." All I knew for certain was that I knew two of the four children's stories, and they were both in heaven with Yeshua; thus, the remaining two children had also to have a story waiting to be told.

As I continued to ponder, I reflected on all the other times a spark of light had mysteriously appeared on the picture. First, a glimmer of light sparked on Sparkle Eyes (a little Asian baby girl). Second, a glimmer sparked on Christopher (my aborted son), and as the dreams continued to come, a sparkle would magically appear on his picture.

With Christopher, the sparkles appeared very randomly, at different times during the period of reoccurring dreams.

So, I walked away from the picture and kept thinking to myself that maybe soon I would have a dream of the little Latino child. Approximately an hour later, I walked back to look at the picture, and still, the magical shimmer dot was shining on the little Latino baby. The shimmering spark had not left. I stared at it for several more minutes and continued wondering, *Why tonight? Why has the shimmering sparkle mysteriously appeared on the back of his head tonight when it has never sparked on him or the fourth child (sex unidentified; at the bottom of the photo) before?*

May 08, 2013

So, without giving it any further thought, I continued with my night as usual. While flipping through the channels, I decided to turn on the nightly news, which was not a regular routine for me and highly unusual because the news always seemed to depress me. However, as soon as I turned to the channel, there was a bright-red heading running across the television screen. The anchorperson began speaking, telling a horrific news-flash story of several women who had been kidnapped by a man named A. Castro in Cleveland, Ohio. The girls had been abducted as very young girls and held captive for several years before one of the girls luckily managed to escape while Castro was away from the house.

Now, honestly, I did not make any connection to the picture sitting by my bedside when I initially started watching the news story. And I almost switched the channel because the news always left me feeling miserable. I continued to watch because I felt sorry for the girls and the story of how one of the girls escaped was truly captivating. I was feeling so happy that they were finally free. So, I continued to watch. I wanted to see how she managed to escape her captor. As the news continued, the stories of all the captive girls were revealed in horrific detail.

I can't remember how many women were held in the home exactly; however, to the best of my recollection, I believe it was a total of three women. One of the women being interviewed identified herself as G. DeJesus. This young lady revealed in horrific detail how she had been beaten repeatedly by Castro. She revealed that she had gotten pregnant by Castro several times and had been forced to have abortions, and I believe, on one occasion, he beat her so bad that she miscarried. She revealed that she had lost five or more children due to being forced to have abortions and/or being badly beaten until she miscarried.

I continued watching the television in disbelief and sadness. I couldn't believe what I was hearing and watching, and suddenly, I looked over at the picture of the four children sitting next to me on my nightstand, the nightstand sitting on the right side of my bed. And oh, my goodness, the shimmering sparkle was shining super brightly on the back of the little Latino child's head. I stood up with my eyes fixated on the picture and stared at it in utter shock, eyes popping out of my head, mouth hanging open. I shouted, "God, he's talking to me, he's talking to me; it's him, it's him! It's his mother. She's his mother!"

I continued running around my room, shouting and jumping in pure joy. God did it; He did it! He really sent me the answer to another child's story; another child in the photo had a story that had just been revealed to me. And just one hour prior to me turning to the news station and this story airing, the shimmer, the glittering sparkle was already shining brightly on the head of the little Latino child. I was completely ecstatic: it was true—he was talking to me; he was telling me it was his turn to reveal his story. His story was being revealed. As I sat there listening to the biggest news story of the evening, I was numb. It was real: the picture was prophetic; the card was God's prophetic message sent to me from the priests, from heaven. God sent the picture to me to reveal each child's story to the world. The message was that they were real people, real human beings, and really were in heaven with God.

I cannot describe on this paper the elation and emotions I experienced as I watched the little Latino child's story on television. "Wows" and "whoos" and tears of sadness were about the best I could do at that moment.

As G. DeJesus was being interviewed, her name appeared on the screen repeatedly, and the anchorperson speaking to her seemed to repeat her name more than once as well. And that's when the lights in my mind came on:

Yes, that's it: God is trying to tell me something. He is revealing the child's name to me; He's telling me the little boy's name is DeJesus. Yes, that is his name, DeJesus. The child's name was the same as his mother's name. The Holy Spirit had revealed this to me. The child was not given the name of his biological father. Thus, the only father this child has is God, with whom he is now in heaven. Yes, that's his story, and it is a true story. Google it.

Interestingly enough, I never had any inclination to refer to the child as the last name of the father.

PS

A short time later, Castro, the father of DeJesus, died in prison.

In the story of King David in the Bible, David was not allowed to build the temple of God.

David's thoughts turned to building a temple for the Lord. King David sent for the prophet Nathan to reveal that he would build a temple for the Lord God. Initially, Nathan encouraged King David to follow through with his desire to build the temple. Yet, that same night, the word of the Lord came to Nathan, changing their plans: "Go and tell my servant David [notice God still refers to King David as His servant], this is what the LORD says: You are not the one to build me a house to dwell in" (1 Chronicles 17:4, NIV). Notice God says, "Build me a house to dwell in."

In 1 Chronicles 22:8 (NIV), God's reason for this decision is revealed. "You have shed much blood and have fought many wars. You are not to build a house for My Name, because you have shed much blood on the earth in my sight." But God was merciful to David: He still allowed his son to be king and build the temple for God.

In the above story of King David, there are a few correlations (revelations) with DeJesus's story.

Is "the temple where I dwell" the human body also referred to as "God's temple"? Yes.

King David was not allowed to build a house in God's name due to the shedding of much blood. Interestingly, the actual word, "name," appears in the biblical text here.

DeJesus's father (Castro) had shed much blood; thus, God's spirit, which dwells in the child (shown in the picture), affectionately named DeJesus, could not take on the name of his biological father (breaking with the earthly tradition) due to the fact that his earthly father had shed much blood. God named the child, not the earthly mother, who doesn't even know that he exists in heaven.

How the Above Passage Relates to You and Me

Notice God still referred to King David as His servant, although his hands were covered with blood. Thus,

God was still merciful and forgiving to King David,

although he had made many earthly mistakes.

Thus, God shows that He is a forgiving God and that He is good. King David repented of his sins and was still very much loving and loyal to God; thus, he was saved. If King David was still considered worthy of being forgiven and accepted by God, so are you and I worthy of God's love if we repent with a true heart. Meaning: turn away from your life of sin and never look back. God will forgive you (1 Chronicles 17:1–2).

God's Note

Geez, literally, as I sat editing DeJesus's story while watching the Gospel channel, Kerry Pharr's show came on at approximately 12:10 a.m., and the content being discussed was, of course, abortion. A man (a gynecologist) who had performed an abortion and two women who had previously had an abortion were being interviewed. I couldn't make this up. I received it as another *God's note*, being sent to me to let me know that I was on the right path by writing this book. Hallelujah!

One Bible verse condemns those who cause harm to children and never repent; Jesus said the following to those who harm little children or cause them to sin:

And whoso shall receive one such little child

in My name receiveth Me. But whoso shall offend one of these little ones which believe in me, it were better for him that a millstone were hanged about his neck and that he were drowned in the depth of the sea.

Matthew 18:5–6

The Fourth Child's Story

The Fourth Child (Bottom of the Picture)

***_ _**

It is a true story (not a dream).

While watching television, I suddenly started flipping channels (like all previous times) whereby some supernatural happenstance, I ended up on a channel revealing the story of the last child. The little blond Caucasian child is depicted at the bottom of the picture on the card, facing Jesus. I suddenly came upon a family discussing the loss of their son Judson.

This was the last mystery child in the picture whose story had not yet been revealed to me, not until that night.

Judson

[***]

I have looked tirelessly for Judson's story in my notes, and I have not been able to find it. I will have to write Judson's story from my heart and recollection of his story as

197

it was revealed.

One evening, while watching television, a family (mother and father) were discussing a family challenge they were enduring with their child Judson. The mother described Judson as having a very rare disease. I can't recall the name of the disease, but it was the kind of disease no parent wanted his or her baby to have. Judson was a young baby boy still riding in a car seat. The parents had gone through at least two or three years of frequent hospital visits, medications, and treatments for Judson. Judson had blond hair and pretty blue eyes; I believe they were blue. The story was so sad. To see such a sweet, beautiful baby, still smiling and happy, suffer such a debilitating illness was a painful experience. In every scene of the show, whenever the camera landed on Judson, he was either smiling or looking very peaceful.

So, of course, initially, I wasn't thinking about my dreams or my picture from heaven. I was just casually watching television and stumbled upon a sad story with two parents desperately fighting to save their baby son's life. And then it happened! The moment that I suddenly realized what was actually happening.

Judson was riding in the back seat of the car, sitting in his car seat while his parents were driving. The mother began describing how Judson was such a happy baby, always smiling and making everyone happy. And suddenly, the camera flashed from the mother's face, while she was still talking about Judson, to Judson's face as he sat quietly, riding in the back seat. The sun was shining brightly upon his face, and then suddenly, it appeared shining over his face like a halo, soft, subtle, and gentle. Yes, it was a beautiful rainbow covering his face with the sun shining bright behind his head. The rainbow honestly looked like a precious jewel wrapped around his face. I truly can't describe how beautiful the moment was when God's gentle presence appeared on his face. It happened so fast that had I blinked, I would have missed it. Seconds after the rainbow appeared on Judson's face, the camera flashed back to his mother, and her very next words were, "Judson didn't make it; he died." My heart broke in that moment because I wanted him to live. I wanted him to survive.

And, yes, as you may have already guessed, the lights (in my head) came on, and suddenly, I realized that the unexpected rainbow shining on Judson's face for a split second was God speaking. He was revealing to me that Judson was with Him in heaven, even before Judson's mother revealed that Judson had gone to heaven to be with God. Keep in mind: there was not a drop of rain in the sky; the rainbow was God's reflection of light and glass on Judson's face in that special moment.

I immediately looked to my right at the picture sitting next to my bed, and I knew that the final child's story had just been revealed to me. I only knew this because of the supernatural rainbow shining on Judson's face. Interestingly, if you look at the picture, you will see the hidden message. Sparkle Eyes and DeJesus are sitting behind Jesus, facing Judson. Christopher is in Jesus's arms, also facing Judson. Judson is the only child sitting on the opposite side of Jesus, looking at the other three children and Jesus.

Of the four children in the picture, Judson is the only child whose parents were fighting for his life and fighting for him to live. (Granted, if DeJesus's mother actually wanted to have an abortion, which is unknown to me. She might have wanted him to live, but the father forced her to have an abortion.) However, Judson is the only child who didn't die at the hands of his own parents but died a natural death after having lived on the earth for two or three years.

If you look closely at the picture, you will see he is looking up at Jesus and the other children. With that said, it is my belief that the position of each child in the picture is symbolic of their individual journeys. Judson's story began on the earth in the physical realm. The earth is below, and heaven is above; thus, Judson's position in the picture (below the other children) seems to be symbolic of the fact that his story and journey to heaven actually began on the earth, where he physically walked it. The other three children never got a chance to physically walk the earth; thus, their lives (the one to be lived) began in heaven.

The two children behind Jesus looking downward toward Judson were aborted or killed at birth. Christopher, the child sent to me in my dreams, also aborted (murdered by me), is sitting above Judson too. Heaven is above; the earth is below.

The placement of the children in the picture carries meaning and purpose.

CHAPTER 13

HAWAII AND THE TRAGEDY OF THE FIFTH CHILD

Unbeknownst to me at the time, there would be two tragedies during this trip.

+V–

While in Hawaii, visiting my mother for Christmas in 2012 (the actual visitation dates were as follows: December 12, 2012, through December 16, 2012), I was so happy; literally, I felt like the happiest daughter on earth. I was so happy to be in Hawaii in my mother's beautiful home. I was so happy to be spending Christmas with my mom and husband, Don, because she was always a shining light for me, and of all the people I've ever known, her light is the only light that never dimmed for me. Hence, happy or sad or mad, she always showed her love to everyone. Unbeknownst to me, this Christmas would be my last Christmas with her because it would be her last Christmas in the earthly realm.

The Saddest Day of My Life

My mother would die one year later, on October 13, 2013.

My visit to Hawaii, in and of itself, was a prophetic supernatural miracle by God because I had to fight to make this visit possible. God allowed me one last visit with my mother, one last time to see her big beautiful eyes, her warm face, and her warm smile. Life is truly priceless because there is no amount of money that can replace my last visit with her. If it were not for God inspiring and allowing me to make the trip this special year to see her, the loss would have been overwhelmingly crushing to my spirit, mind, body, and soul. And still, it was absolutely devastating.

My advice is to always be on the alert, looking and listening for the whispers of the Holy Spirit. This is what I did when I insisted that Mr. N. and I spend this particular Christmas with my mother instead of his family, which had been our tradition every Christmas. And I almost gave in to Mr. N.'s request to spend another Christmas with his family, but something inside kept nudging me, and the feeling would not let go. Besides, I knew I missed her, and the thought of spending Christmas in beautiful Hawaii was also exhilarating.

The Holy Spirit will speak to you in a number of ways, sometimes with visions, sightings, dreams, physical artifacts, people, animals, birds, wind, inanimate objects, places, children, glitter, crumbs, and honestly, the list is infinite because God is infinite.

Yes, I know this sounds crazy, but imagine yourself a spirit moving about the earth without physical flesh. How would you communicate with your loved ones? Yep, any way you could.

Tragedy Unfolding on the Nightly News:
the Fifth Child's Story

Sandy Hook
:.....|^

The fifth child's face is not on the supernatural card that was sent to me by the priest in 2012, as he was still alive at this time.

An important note: this child's story was completely unexpected and, as far as I know, unprecedented in the United States.

Now that I knew the stories of all the children on the supernatural card sent to me by God, I thought, *Okay, that is it. The end.* Boy, was I wrong; there would be another child's story imminently!

While in Hawaii, relaxing on my mother's cushy recliner chair, I witnessed all the news channels begin to flood the television with the following headline: *"Breaking News."*

It was a live story, a tragedy unfolding on all the television-network news channels.

On Friday, December 14, 2012 (Hanukkah), there was a mass shooting at Sandy Hook Elementary School in Newtown, Connecticut. The story was still developing, and many details were still unknown, but so far, what I could gather was a gunman named Long opened fire on several young people, including young children between the ages of six and seven, and some adults, killing twenty-six people in total.

I sat looking at the television, completely desolated and in shock, with my eyes fixed on the television screen. What kind of animal could do such as beastly, savage, and terrible, horrific thing to such beautiful little children? The last thing I saw on the television before turning in for bed that evening was several desperate parents standing outside the school, waiting for the news about their child and if he/she had been saved.

This tragic scene carried well into the late-night hours and continued for several days as the police worked tirelessly, searching for survivors and identifying the children who had perished in the terrible murderous rampage of a devil. Night had fallen, and still, none of the victims had been identified, at least not publically. It was a very sad, heartbreaking scene to watch. My mother and I were both devastated. I was so desperately horrified I decided to resign for the evening.

That Night: the Tenth Supernatural Prophetic Dream

Christopher's voice came to me in my last and final dream of him.

This was the first time he ever spoke to me audibly.

:.........|

On Saturday, December 15, 2012, while I was sleeping, Christopher's voice came to me in a dream. He said the following words: "Christopher has a new friend, *B*." And I awoke. That was all he said, and that was the last time he visited me in a dream.

I was absolutely fascinated that he had come to me again, although this time very briefly; I was still ecstatic that he came to me in another dream. Whenever God, Jesus, and the Holy Spirit allowed Christopher to visit me in a dream, I knew it was a blessing and a gift from God, for which I was truly grateful and undeserving. I awoke, very excited about my dream. I couldn't wait to tell my mother. Due to the fact that I had not dreamed of him for several months, I began to wonder, *Why now? Why did he come now? Maybe he wants me to know that he is here with me.*

Still a little sleepy, I yawned and took in a deep breath of the fresh morning air coming in through a vent in the ceiling. There was simply no air like the clean, warm breezy air of Hawaii's fresh sunshiny mornings.

While sitting there, I began pondering the dream. What did it mean? What did Christopher mean when he said,

"Christopher has a new friend, *B*"? *Hum*, I sat thinking, *What was the initial B?* So, I started thinking, *Can it be that one of the children's names began with the letter B? Huh, that's it; maybe that's what he meant!*

I jumped up out of bed and ran into the living room where my mother was sitting, having her morning cup of coffee and, like always, watching Fox News, her and Don's favorite news station. The news everywhere was covering the deadly incident that took place in Sandy Hook.

I looked at my mother and asked, "Mom, did any of the children have a name that began with the letter *B*?" She looked at me and replied, "Morning, Taylor. I am not sure." Of course, I was devastated at what had happened in Sandy Hook, so I knew the only way I would be able to find out the names of all the children who had been killed was to sit and watch the entire news story for myself. So, I sat down at the beautiful large light-oak wooden table and began watching the news coverage of one of the worse events to occur in US history.

And I thought it would be a while before the names of the kids started appearing on the television; however, it didn't happen like that. As soon as I started watching, the sad and devastating images of some of the children who had been identified started flashing across the television screen. It was an absolute nightmare to see their innocent faces and the absolute devastation caused by one, still unidentified, man. As I sat watching, my eyes filled with tears, so the screen was blurry.

For that reason, even to this very day, I cannot remember the names of any of the children, that is, except for one. I somehow knew without a shadow of a doubt that the name of one of the children would start with the letter *B* because of my dream. So far, everything that happened in the dreams had proven to be true and real.

And suddenly, he appeared. That was the name, the child whose name began with the letter *B*. Christopher's new friend in heaven. And there he was, his face so friendly, so happy, and humble looking. I could tell he was a darling child for his parents. He wore a green-and-white striped shirt. And then his name appeared. It was Benjamin. Benjamin was Christopher's new friend in heaven.

I was in absolute awe. It was another confirmation that heaven is real, and for the first time, my son spoke to me, and I understand why. It was the only way he could reveal Benjamin was his new friend. Remember, none of the other children's faces in heaven were revealed to me. I could hear their laughter, but I could not see their faces. I believe this is because their stories do not belong to me and are being hidden (held) until their stories are revealed to those whom God has chosen for them. Hopefully, their own parents. At the time, I didn't know this would be Christopher's last visit, but it was.

Jesus allowed Christopher to return to me one last time to reveal that he had a new friend in heaven named *B*.

Although the dreams stopped that December, I continued to see and experience supernatural miracles, signs, and wonders.

Benjamin, the fifth child (face deliberately not shown):

The Next Day

While dining at a bar with Mr. N., I began talking to a random stranger, and we were both just speaking about how happy and fortunate we felt to be living in Hawaii and/or have people who lived here who we could visit. As I began introducing myself, I asked the stranger his name, and he replied, "Josh." We continued briefly with the conversation, and then he looked to his right and said, "This is my friend." I replied, "Oh, nice to meet you. What's your name?" He replied, "Benjamin." I immediately noticed his name and that he was sitting to the right side of Josh.

It wasn't much of a jaw-dropping "wow" at the moment because I was not thinking deeply enough about it since we were at dinner, having a strawberry margarita. However, sometime later, while writing this chapter of the book, I was searching through my phone, looking for notes, pictures, and videos that had been stored in preparation for the book. And actually, I believe I was looking for Benjamin's photo, the one that I had captured from the nightly news while I was in Hawaii.

And like all the other supernatural occurrences, one of the first videos I happened to stumble upon was the video with the two friends, Josh and Benjamin, who lived in Hawaii. Had I not stumbled on this video and watched it again, I would have totally missed the hidden message sent to me that evening through the subtle whisper of the Holy Spirit confirming that my dream was real and that Benjamin was in heaven with my son Christopher. Benjamin is the only child's name sent to me in that dream.

Irony or coincidence? You tell me.

Supernatural Moment at Fox Hills Park on March 20, 2013

Real-Life Event (Fox Hills Park)

<3 I >3

While jogging at the park, as usual, I stopped to use a workout machine for the legs. And suddenly, for no apparent reason, I began thinking of my son Christopher. I started sadly longing for him. So, I stopped running, stood still, and closed my eyes. With my eyes closed tightly, I imagined myself in a field of purple lilies. I had a vision of my son Christopher running toward me in the field of purple lilies. He was wearing all white. I stretched out my arms toward him (literally, in real life, I also had my arms opened) as he continued running to me. My eyes were still closed. And then I opened my eyes from the vision in my mind.

When I opened my eyes (I promise, I couldn't make this up), there was a little boy (approximate age five or six) running across the large field of grass at Fox Hills Park. He was running directly toward me. He was a little Latino boy wearing a blue hat. I watched him run toward me and smiled. My smile got bigger and bigger as he made it closer to me. I couldn't believe what I was seeing: there was a little boy running forward, as though he was running to me. He had almost made it to me when he stopped by a tree right in front of me where his dad had accidentally hit the baseball all the way across the field from where they were playing (approximately more than sixty feet). I knew this was no mistake or coincidence at all. It was God; it was God. As I watched the little boy run back to his father, I took a moment to say, "Thank You, Christ, and thank you, Christopher."

Let God, Yeshua, and the Holy Spirit take you back to school so that you too can know the truth. I beseech you to refuse to follow the blind.

"They are blind leaders of the blind. And if the blind leads the blind, both shall fall into a ditch" (Matthew 15:14, NKJV).

When Jesus spoke, He frequently spoke in parables, especially when delivering hidden messages, secrets, and truths that needed to be revealed to His disciples.

After I read the card front to back, I perceived God's subliminal message to me as follows: God, Jesus, and the Holy Spirit would be teaching me something new, something I did not know, educating me about something that is of critical concern to God, and revealing a hidden truth to me that also needed to be revealed to the world. Hence, the title of the card: "Best wishes for being back to school." What happens when we go back to school? School is where knowledge is passed from the teacher to the student.

CHAPTER 14

THE SUPERNATURAL SONG

<> v <>

One day, while I was listening to the radio, one of my favorite female singers came on air, singing a beautiful sad melody. The song came on supernaturally while I was listening to music on my iPhone. The song was one that I had enjoyed listening to as a college student. Honestly, as a child, I am sure I might have heard some of the Carpenters' songs played by my schoolteachers and mother. However, as an adult (beyond college), I rarely listened to the Carpenters. For this reason, I know that God (Yahweh), Jesus (Yeshua), and the Holy Spirit led me to the Carpenters, who began singing a very special song. After I finished listening to the popular song by the Carpenters that I liked so much, I decided to continue listening to the other songs on the album. And suddenly, a song that I had never heard before began playing. I could not believe my ears. God led me to this truly special song, where a woman with the voice of an angel (Karen Carpenter) began singing.

This song was definitely intended for me to hear. The lyrics were so in-line with all of my dreams I knew it was meant for me to receive. While listening, I cried and wept sadly because every word in the song was so true and so real. The moment it came on was truly supernatural, so supernatural I just sat crying.

"Bless the Beasts and the Children"

Here is a snapshot of the supernatural song that gives you part of God's answer to abortion. He hears and sees *all*, including the silent cries of the souls of innocent babies as they are being mercilessly killed in the wombs of their mothers.

"Bless the beasts and children; for in this world, they have no voice, they have no choice" (Carpenters, "Bless the Beasts and the Children," 1971).

Listen to the Children

It is definitely not irony or coincidence that the first line of the song is, "Bless the beasts and children; for in this world, they have no voice, they have no choice."

There is no word in the Hebrew Bible for "irony" or "coincidence."

The major theme of Planned Parenthood and abortion-right advocates is "woman's choice."

After hearing this song, I fully came to understand my God-given assignment. God wanted me to be "their voice." The voice of the children who have been thrown away as meaningless garbage.

They may not have mattered to you and me, but they mattered to God as much then as they do now. And one day, this will all be revealed to you in one way or another.

The Supernatural Balloon Shapes and Figures

(*)

During the time I was having all the dreams and visions, I also began noticing that I kept seeing the same recurring image throughout my house, in various forms. A recurring figure usually appeared in my bathroom sink while I was doing my hair. I always spent a lot of time in my bathroom. The image was the shape of a balloon on a string. At first, I paid no attention to it and simply wiped it (usually made of hair that had fallen in the sink) off the sink or floor, wherever it was lying. But after I started seeing the same image again and again everywhere in my house, I started to take notice, especially considering all that I had been going through with the dreams and supernatural experiences. So, I began to wonder why I was seeing this image so frequently and if it could also be a sign from God trying to tell me something.

It looked like the shape of a balloon. What possible significance could a balloon have? And then the lights came on, *That's it: kids like balloons. Yes, that's it. Christopher wants me to blow up some balloons.* So, I started blowing up balloons and letting them flow freely throughout my house. I began to notice how they moved so subtly with the wind. *Wow,* I thought, *Can it be that my breath in the balloon is God's breath in the balloon, my soul that cannot be seen or touched but is captured in the balloon?*

Yes, that's it. God wanted me to understand that the breath in my body was my soul breathing; hence His breath, which is life, and the only way any human being on this earth can live is with God's breath breathed into their bodies. The balloon was symbolic of the human body with God's breath breathed into it, thus my soul, my life. Without my breath being blown into the balloon, the balloon would have remained still and lifeless, but once I filled it with my breath, hence air, it came to life and could move freely throughout the house just like a living soul, and it didn't need me to push it because the wind (small, subtle wind) made it move. Thus, maybe this is how our souls move (free like the wind) once the material flesh is gone. No man knows this answer yet.

From that day on, I continued blowing up balloons in my home and sometimes in the homes of others (in spite of their laughter) because, honestly, I believed Christopher just might see them and feel my love for him because I complied with God's nudging to blow up balloons. And on occasion, without me expecting or noticing the balloon was close to me, one would float past my feet or drift near my bedside without me ever touching them.

I know what you may be thinking, but remember there are no limitations with God; all things are possible with Him.

Christopher's Parents

(-)

Finding Physical Artifacts, Objects, and Mysterious Sightings

<*>

This is the second mysterious image that I happened to come upon while walking. This picture reveals a perfectly formed shadow of a fish shape on the ground. I could tell it had not been drawn with any sort of chalk or marker. It was right there in front of me as I was walking.

The Fish Shadow on the Concrete

Bathroom Trash-Can Picture

One day, while attempting to empty the trash, I looked down and saw a face made of trash that I had thrown away earlier that day. See the eyes made of the tealight candles. See the white tissue in the middle of the tealight candles. I know you may feel it's a stretch, but if God can use a burning bush to speak to Moses, He can use trash in a trash can to speak to me. And besides, isn't that what I did to my son when I aborted him—threw him in the trash?

Cloud-Figure Picture

Look at the *cloudlike figure* behind Donovan's head. If you look closely at the top left side of the picture, behind Donovan's head, you will see a cloudlike figure looking down at Donovan. The cloudlike figure is a face made of clouds. The figure has two eyes, a very tiny nose, and a mouth in the shape of a triangle or diamond. Now look a little closer, just under the face in the cloud, on the far-left side; you will see a small heart with an arrow pointing down toward Donovan. This picture was not this way when it was originally taken. I am still not sure how the picture came to have the cloudlike figure on it, but it did.

Picture of a Happy Face Made of Dish Suds

In 2012, while I was washing dishes, one of the pots revealed a hidden gem. Look for yourselves; what do you see? Yes, that is what I see too. It looks like a face made of clouds to me.

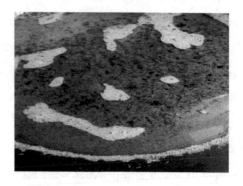

CHAPTER 15

THE PICTURE OF HER GOODBYE...

October 2013

...and she left

My Mother Died on October 13, 2013

:(0--

One thing I did on my final visit to see my mother at her home in Hawaii in 2012 was that I told her about the dreams I had of my aborted son Christopher, whom I met in heaven. After telling her of the very special dreams and experiences, I decided to show her the magic of balloons.

So, I went about the house, blowing up balloon after balloon. Once I had finished blowing them up, I released them to flow freely throughout the house. Most importantly, I wanted her to see how the balloons moved in a majestic way with the wind. I also wanted to see if the balloons would move about her house as they did mine. Somehow, at least one of the balloons would magically end up somewhere near me. Sometimes a balloon would brush across my feet. It didn't seem to matter where the balloons had been placed in the home; at least one would find its way to me. I felt in my heart that the Holy Spirit was sending me a message from heaven to let me know that Christopher loved me and was near.

And of course, my mom would give me a little funny chuckle and glance; you know, the kind that parents sometimes give children who still believe in magic. But in my heart, I felt somehow she believed me. I knew deep down inside that she believed in God and His miracles and that He could still send us signs from heaven because He is pure light, grace, and endless love.

Fast-Forward to the Next Year, 2013

The morning of my mother's funeral, which was the saddest day of my entire life, I awoke and rolled over on my right side after letting out a deep sigh of pure indescribable sadness. I couldn't believe that just one year prior, I had laid in that same bed, sucking in all the beauty of the sunny-morning Hawaiian breeze.

When I rolled over onto my right side, I looked up, and there was a small diamond-shaped figure on the wall, sitting right next to me. I just stared at it for several minutes in utter sadness, crying my heart out, knowing that, somehow, this diamond-shaped figure, one that I had never ever seen before, during any of my trips to visit her, had to be a message from God, from her, from heaven, letting me know that she was okay and that she was in heaven in the brilliant light of God.

I tell you the truth: I never ever saw this figure or any other figure on any of the walls in her house until that day, that morning, the morning of her funeral. I was so sad that I could not muster the feeling of awe in my broken heart, but deep down inside, I know I was truly amazed.

Sail on, Mom

8

∧

I have one last thing to say in relation to my mother's passing.

Birds Are God's Messengers

<I>

On the day of my mother's viewing, which lasted approximately three hours, I drove into the mortuary parking structure and randomly pulled into an empty parking space. I was so saddened and overwhelmed with unbearable grief that I barely had any sort of consciousness, especially of anything around me. However, the bird that just happened to be sitting on the chain-linked fence directly above my car's front window briefly caught my eye as I exited the vehicle to go into the mortuary to see my mother's physical flesh on this earth for one last time.

Occasionally, while still inside the mortuary, I would glance outside and notice the bird sitting in the same spot right above my car on the chain-link fence. Not that I was really concerned about looking for the bird, but I needed to look away from my mother lying there helpless. Or maybe I felt helpless.

I promise you, three hours later, when I returned to my car after saying goodbye to my mother, the bird was still there, sitting on the fence in the same spot: right above my car. Was she here with us, looking down on us? I believe she was.

Meet the Bird

Meet the bird sitting on the fence outside the mortuary of my mother's memorial service.

Finding Heavenly Artifacts

The following artifacts were found in different locations at different times, most while I was walking outside my apartment, which was much like a large green leafy forest with tall trees everywhere. Like with all the dreams, visions, and supernatural wonders, I know that these artifacts were sent to me by God, Yeshua, and the Holy Spirit.

I believe the heavenly artifacts were purposely placed in my pathway by the Holy Spirit so that there would be no possible way of me missing them. The heart made of mud and red clay or brick was sitting right in the middle of the walkway one late afternoon as I returned home from an evening stroll. The perfectly rounded thorny branch, in like manner, was sitting right in the middle of the walkway as I found it. They were very conspicuous. And why didn't someone else find them? Why me? Those two questions are what helped me understand that they were supernaturally meant to be found by me.

And again, like all the other wonders, finding the heavenly artifacts was totally unexpected and awe-provoking.

Priceless Artifacts

1. Perfectly formed heart made of mud, earth, or dirt on one side and some form of brick material, the color of deep crimson red, like the color of blood, on the other side.
2. Perfectly formed crown of thorns (in appearance).
3. Perfectly formed fish shadow on the ground.

A symbol of a jagged-looking cross made of wood.

The front side of the heart is made of dirt from the earth:

The back side of the heart is made of crimson-red brick material:

To see the true brilliance and color of the precious heavenly artifact, go to Instagram @godsanswertoabortion.

Galactic Keyhole

A special ring with a mysterious hidden message came to me in a dream.

The picture of the symbol of a *key like a cross* came to me in a dream. The image in my dream was the symbol of a cross with a circle on top. As I later discovered, it is called the ankh or "key of life" cross symbol. It is considered an ancient Egyptian hieroglyphic symbol that was most commonly used in writing and in Egyptian art to represent the word for "life" by extension and as a symbol of life itself.

Many years later, while watching a television documentary, I discovered that there is a scientific study of the same exact shape I saw in my dreams (cross with a circle on top) that looks much like the shape of a keyhole called the galactic keyhole. This symbol is considered to be an unsolved mystery that has been discovered in many ancient locations around the world, including India, China, and even on the moon.

However, in the documentary, they didn't include a location where I believe I have also seen the same shape appear. Sometime later, I watched a documentary about the Dead Sea Scrolls, which I believe were first discovered in Egypt in 1945 by a couple of men. While watching this documentary, which revealed real footage of the site where the scrolls were discovered, I know with absolute certainty, I also saw the mysterious shape known as the galactic keyhole, hidden in a section of the mountains surrounding the cave where the Dead Sea Scrolls were discovered. Google it.

I am still fascinated with the mystery of the galactic keyhole because the mystery remains unsolved. It is my belief that the mystery leads to a hidden message from God and Yeshua, which has yet to be revealed to the world. Why was it sent to me as part of a series of dreams if it didn't carry a significant meaning?

Refer to the Instagram account @Godsanswertoabortion to see the image of the cross and/or keyhole I saw in my dream.

Heaven and Hell

The Fourth Messenger

Bob Jones

=++=

Sunday, December 2018

This messenger came a few years after all the dreams of my son Christopher stopped occurring and a few years after my mother died.

While flipping religious channels, I came across a show titled *Heaven and Hell*, so naturally, after all my dreams, I was very curious. It was on channel 365, and the network title only showed one word, "God." The full name of the television network was God TV. So, I clicked on the channel, and immediately, I saw two men sitting at a table, talking. One man was interviewing the other. Both of the men had white or gray hair. The man being interviewed was Prophet Bob Jones, who was recounting his experience of going to heaven and hell after falling into a deep sleep. He had been taken to both heaven and hell over a series of dreams.

The thing that immediately caught my attention was the year of the interview. While Bob was speaking, I heard him say, "This year, 2013, is the beginning of the harvest, the unending harvest to come." My mother died on October 13, 2013. He said we began to come into this realm in

2012. Thus, he was being interviewed sometime in 2013. Now, according to the date the show first aired (Saturday, December 17, 2016), and it was reaired again on Sunday, December 18, I have deduced that I must have also recorded it in 2016. Unfortunately, the actual date of the interview (the month in 2013) was not made public, but I have calculated the actual date of the interview might have been in December of 2013.

Unfortunately, Bob Jones died a year after the interview in 2014.

While watching the interview, I realized that I had tuned into the show late, so I missed the first half, where Bob described the first part of his dream, where the Holy Spirit took him to hell. The part I was able to catch was where he described being in a dark tunnel. He described seeing two lines and described himself as being all light. The man guiding him was also made of white light; this reminded me of the angel who I saw floating through my home right before I started having all the dreams of heaven. She was made of pure-white translucent material that glowed.

When Bob walked out of the dark tunnel, per his description, he as if stepped into a bright light, which was revealed to be the love of God. He indicated that the light was the glory of God, so beautiful that he was unable to describe the beauty of the light.

He indicated that there were two lines, where one line didn't have that many people, and the other line, to the left, was long and had many people standing in it. Those people were described as people who didn't know the Lord and chose to never know Him. The Holy Spirit then said to Bob that everyone in that line had a choice and that they had made their choice on the earth. The line with the people going to heaven was only 2 percent of the entire human population, and Bob was in that line. In the other line, people were covered with darkness; they did not have light on them at all. That line was much longer than the line Bob was in.

I tuned in just in time to hear his account of his trip to heaven (Thanks, Yeshua, Yahweh, and the Holy Spirit). However, what stood out the most to me about this interview were the words Bob said once he was out of the tunnel of darkness leading to the light. Once out of the tunnel of darkness, he entered a place with a bright light where he saw a man that he described as God with His arms wide open. While looking at the line facing God, he saw the first person in the line of light was a large Black woman. Bob said God looked at the woman as she stood before Him and asked her one question, "Did you learn to love?" The women looked at God and answered, "Yes, Lord, I did." And the woman walked into His arms and into the light.

Now, this might not sound like such a big deal, but trust me when I say it was a very wonderful supernatural moment for me. The reason I say this is because throughout my mother's life, from her childhood, she had difficulty with her weight and self-image. She always felt like she was overweight and was very insecure about her weight. Thus, she always felt like a large Black woman. And I truly believe that at one point in my life, I actually heard her refer to herself in the same manner, "large Black woman." So, the fact that Bob used the word "large" and not just "Black woman" (which could have been any Black woman) made me truly believe that the woman he saw walking into the arms of God was indeed my mother. It felt like God had given Bob the coded language that would signal to me that the woman in the story was my mother.

My mother died in 2013, and I believe some of Bob's dreams of heaven occurred in that same year. He could have used the word "Black" without using the word "large," but the fact that he used the word "large" made me realize this was a message sent to me by the Holy Spirit from my mom letting me know that she had made it into heaven. Keep in mind: I was just randomly flipping through channels and just happened to come upon the channel at the moment Bob began describing his trip to heaven and the large Black woman.

While listening to him describe his trip to heaven, I sat in awe and amazement with my mouth hanging wide. I could not believe what I was hearing. So, it was definitely no mistake or coincidence that I turned to that channel at the exact moment that he was talking about being taken to heaven, where he saw two lines, one with those going to heaven and one with those going to hell. And how is it that the very first person he saw walking into God's arms in heaven was the "large Black woman"?

There is no word for "coincidence" in the Hebrew Bible.

Please believe me when I tell you that God is real, heaven is real, and hell is real.

CHAPTER 16

DO YOU BELIEVE IN ANGELS?

Dream of the Angel Made of Clouds,
Blowing a Horn, with a Rainbow

In 2012, I had a prophetic dream of an angel floating on clouds, in front of a rainbow, blowing a horn.

The Bible describes the end of days this way: "So, the seven angels who had the seven trumpets prepared themselves to sound" (Revelation 8:6, NKJV).

I believe this dream was a prophetic, revelatory dream of things to come in the end. An angel or guide who I could not see walked along my side and guided me down a long, dark, dilapidated-looking road until we came to the end of the road. It was covered with dust, deep-dark gray-looking dust, and dirt everywhere.

Remember how the streets looked on the day of September 11, 2001? This is how the entire road we walked on looked but even darker because the entire sky was dark. It was a dark night, and there were wrecked-looking cars along the road. The cars looked inoperable, broken down, and abandoned. The cars were not parked in any specific order but were scattered about and very few. There was no one else on the road other than the angel guiding me and me. I didn't see any human beings anywhere. When we reached the end of the road where we could walk no further, my guide and I stopped and looked up at the sky, and there was an angel in the clouds. The angel was made completely of white or transparent cloudlike material. He was completely surrounded by clouds as though embedded in them. He held a horn in his hands. The horn appeared similar to a trumpet but was very straight and smooth with no handles or added parts. I believe it might have been the color of gold, but I can't remember this detail for sure. The angel's head was tilted slightly upward, pointing toward the sky above it, with the horn pointing at a forty-five-degree angle.

The angel appeared to be blowing the horn. The bed of clouds was positioned slightly behind the angel, and there was a beautiful rainbow that stretched the entire length of the clouds from the left side to the right side. The rainbow was built directly into the clouds and sat just behind the angel's head but slightly higher than the angel. It was truly an amazing sight to behold. I awoke.

Yeshua, thank You for this dream. You are truly *awesome* and *amazing*!

The picture above attempts to illustrate the image of the angel I saw in my dream; however, it is a far cry from the true beauty of the angel made of light and cloudlike material, embedded in a bed of clouds with a bright, colorful rainbow nestled behind his head. I do not believe I could ever truly describe the beauty of the angel in the clouds.

The photo (featured above) was taken by Mr. N.'s daughter sometime in 2012. The photo contains a mysterious rainbow embedded in the clouds, stretching across the sky. I believe it was taken after a light rainfall in 2012, around the same time I was having the prophetic supernatural dreams. The rainbow in my dream looked almost exactly like the rainbow in the photo taken in 2012, except there was no angel embedded in the middle of the clouds. However, in hindsight, I do believe there might have been an angel in the clouds on the day the real-life photo was taken; we just couldn't see him.

The color version of the photo of the clouds with the embedded rainbow is much more illustrious and beautiful than the one depicted here. To see the original photo of the rainbow embedded in the clouds, visit our Instagram page @godsanswertoabortion.

The interesting correlation is Mr. N.'s daughter might have been the person to photograph the clouds with the mysterious rainbow, and in one of my dreams of my son Christopher in heaven, she was the one who spoke and revealed that Christopher was her brother. The picture was so beautiful Mr. N. decided to show it to me. I do not believe this was a coincidence at all.

In 2012, one year before my mother died, while I was visiting her for what would become our last Christmas together, I went out for dinner and drinks at an outdoor restaurant; this bird sat next to me for several minutes without moving.

One day, I asked two self-professed God-fearing Christians a question, "What do you think about abortion?"

The man replied, "I don't know. I don't really get involved in all that stuff."

The woman replied, "It is the woman's body, so it is the woman's choice."

I walked away sad because I realized that both had been blinded by the messages of the blind. Neither seemed to realize that because they refused to choose life, they had actually chosen death. Not only for the child in the mother's womb but also for themselves.

It was at that moment that I knew it was imperative that I write this book and that I write it quickly.

"Hearts of stone, hearts of steel refuse to see what is real," the Holy Spirit once said to me.

Jesus said, "I will lead the blind by ways they have not known, along unfamiliar paths I will guide them; I will turn the darkness into light before them and make the rough places smooth" (Isaiah 42:16, NIV).

In case you are still scratching your heads or confused about what God's answer to abortion is, as it was revealed to me by the Holy Spirit, the answer is revealed in the remaining chapters of this book.

The quote is provided by Abigail Holt as she was speaking to Marilyn and Sarah about her new book on the Daystar network station. The quote sums up much of what I have come to know about God. He can speak to us in a variety of ways, and sometimes His voice is so subtle that if you blink, you will miss it.

"The Kingdom of God is so simple; you could miss it," said Abigail Holt (*Today with Marilyn and Sarah*, Daystar, 2021).

The next few pages will uncover a few real-life events, correlations, and mysterious, peculiar happenings that were revealed to me by the Holy Spirit.

All of the mysterious occurrences revealed…

God's Voice as It Whispers

God can use several methods to communicate His desires and messages to us. There are several examples of this in the Bible: the burning bush and Moses, the plagues that were released on the Egyptians for refusing to release the Israelites, the tiny cloud in the sky during the years of drought, confirming Elijah's proclamation of supernatural rain to come, and last but not least, Jonah in the belly of the whale. In this instance, God used a whale to get Jonah's attention and redirect him back to Nineveh to complete his assignment (Jonah 1–2).

See a few interesting correlations God revealed to me. There is no word for "coincidence" in the Hebrew Bible; thus, I accept all mysterious (unexplainable) occurrences as God speaking to me, God's voice, God's answer. God's math is exact, not wavering or changing.

Fun Fact of Physics

There are numbers that men cannot see or count or calculate; these numbers are known as the God numbers.

The First Documentary: Einstein

"I want to know God's thoughts in a mathematical way" (Albert Einstein).

$E = Mc2$

Energy (unseen) = God's breath

Material content (seen) = physical (i.e., the human bodies)

2 = squared (energy becomes material content, and material content returns to energy)

This is the cycle of life as described by God in the Bible. Einstein is the physicist who I believe captured the essence of the cycle of life through the equation $E = Mc^2$.

Could this be the reason this documentary was brought to my attention?

The equation revealed the following to me: energy becomes material content, and material content returns to energy, which usually cannot be seen with the naked eye but is present everywhere in the atmosphere.

Was God using a documentary about a world-famous physicist to reveal to me a hidden message that all life begins as energy (God's breath)?

Even if there is no noticeable heartbeat in the mother's womb, *God's breath* is there in the mother's womb as a *living soul*. Just as there are prime numbers on the number chart that cannot be seen by the eye of man or calculated by the hand or computer of man, God can see them and knows that the numbers are there.

Even though we, mothers, cannot see or feel the babies in our wombs at the initial stages of their conception, God can see them; He knows them, and He knows that they are there.

CHAPTER 17

THE BALLOONS

One evening, the Holy Spirit guided me to blow up a balloon (breathe air into a balloon). Initially, I didn't understand why, but hindsight is a twenty-twenty vision. Now that I think back on it, I realize the Holy Spirit was guiding me to understand how and when life begins in the mother's womb. Life begins with the unseen supernatural breath of God.

In essence, life is God's breath (unseen) planted in the womb of the mother at the time of the soul's conception. This is the initial stage of human development. Since the (physical) seed of life (sperm) comes from a man, when it enters the egg in the womb of the mother is when life begins.

During the time I was having all the dreams and experiencing mysterious sightings, I began noticing a peculiar image, a recurring image that was popping up everywhere, usually in my sink while I was doing my hair or grooming myself (focusing on me). The image looked like a balloon on a string. At first, I paid no attention to it, but after I continued seeing the same image again and again, all over my house (sometimes in the kitchen, sometimes on the floor, or sink), I began to take notice and wonder why I was seeing this image so frequently. After looking back at everything that happened over the course of the last few years, I came to realize that the Holy Spirit was sending me a new message. *Balloons*, I thought, *That is it: Christopher wants balloons.*

God wanted me to blow up some balloons. I really couldn't think of a reason why God would want me to do this until one late afternoon while I was having a conversation with my cousin about his mother, who had cancer. I was trying to think of a way that he could continue to be comforted when she passes from the physical realm (earth) to the unseen energy field (second heaven). So, I asked him to have his terminally ill mother blow up a balloon for him so that he would always have a part of her (her breath) stored in a balloon that he could keep with him forever. God was trying to show me something.

However, long before this conversation, I had already started blowing up balloons (as instructed by God). I began placing them all around my house. And sometimes, I would sit and watch them float freely. I began noticing the subtle way in which they moved about the house. They moved in a playful fashion and sometimes appeared to take on a life of their own, moving about the house like a child at play, running, laughing, and singing. It became a beautiful sight for me to watch them move.

The Bamboo Trees

Bamboo trees, like fetuses growing inside their mother's womb, remain hidden in the earth (their womb) for five years before physically manifesting on the surface. While in the earth, although it cannot be seen, a bamboo tree is totally alive from the time the seed is planted in the earth. Like a baby in the womb of its mother, the bamboo tree remains in the womb of the earth, living, breathing, and growing until it is time to spring forward from the earth to thrive and manifest physically. Once it emerges from the womb of the earth, it will grow ninety feet tall within five weeks.

The Breath of God Was Breathed into the Nostrils of Man

"Then the Lord God formed man from the dust of the ground and breathed into his nostrils the breath of life, and the man became a living soul" (Genesis 2:7, NIV).

Life begins with the breath of God.

The soul is God's breath. The soul is the living organism, seed, in the mother's womb before there is a physical manifestation (parts of the body begin to form).

God Is Life

God's breath comes before physical manifestation. God's breath is life. A body (flesh) without God's breath (the soul) is dead, but a soul without a body is still alive.

God's breath is in every fiber and tiny particle (star-dust) that comes together to form the beautiful physical flesh that we, humans, become. His breath is in every tiny heart (the heart that is beating in the mother's womb) that can first be scientifically detected at six weeks' gestation in the mother's womb.

But God already knows it's there before science knows.

The Two-Day Abortion: a Friend's True Story

Warning: graphic detail.

The story you are about to hear is a true, real-life story, an unfiltered depiction of a two-day abortion procedure. I have purposely included the raw details of what I was told about the procedure experienced by my friend. I have also included what I deduced from pure common sense and basic science after hearing my friend's story (i.e., the pure agony of pouring salt onto an open wound).

First of all, what is a two-part abortion? A two-part abortion is a second-trimester abortion that is usually performed between fourteen to twenty-three and a half weeks of pregnancy. This type of abortion requires one to three visits to the abortion clinic. The procedure used in this type of abortion is known as dilation and evacuation. The abortion clinics can and sometimes do use medication to prepare the cervix instead of dilators. Let me make it clear because the abortion clinics hide the truth of the matter by using deceptive language such as "gentle suctioning," "cervical softening," "small dilating sticks."

The Truth in Layman's Terms

- Those small dilating sticks are not only used to soften or widen your cervix, but they are also killing the fetus that is alive, breathing, and well in the uterus.
- The small dilating sticks, while dilating the cervix, also assist in killing the fetus on day one, when it is still in the womb. On day two, the mother returns to the clinic, and the fetus (alive or dead) is suctioned out of the womb.

Why Use Seaweed Dilating Sticks?

On day one, the baby, fetus, is still alive in the womb and is a nice size already.

If the seaweed dilating sticks were not inserted into the mother's womb to help widen, open, and soften the cervix and kill the living baby in the mother's womb, the doctors would most likely have to hear and face the music of the murders they are committing.

A baby crying for its life.

Yes, a crying, screaming baby as its body is being crushed to death by a medical suctioning device (tool of death), basically a vacuum cleaner.

- And about those small dilating sticks made of seaweed or a seaweed-like substance. Do you know what seaweed does to a body without skin or a body with very sensitive skin?
- Have you ever witnessed someone pouring salt on a snail without its shell?
- Have you ever tried pouring salt on a fresh cut or open wound on your body?

Yes, that is what the unborn fetus feels when the seaweed sticks are stuck into the mother's uterus, like a snail whose extremely soft shell-less body feels when salt hits it (burning, bubbling, and blistering until it disintegrates and dies).

The fetus in the womb experiences the same until it ultimately dies.

This procedure is so evil and so cruel I could barely type the details of it on this page. First, they kill the child to silence it, dehumanize it, and make it no more than a routine surgical procedure to be performed. Afterward, the tiny broken pieces of the baby's body are thrown away; that is, whatever part is not used for selling or scientific research. As for the mother: as described to me by my friend, on day one of the procedure, she went home with the seaweed sticks in her cervix, uterus. She described the extreme pain as almost unbearable. The pain felt like severe cramping all through the night. She indicated that she was in so much pain from the cramping and gas bubbles moving around in her stomach she was unable to sleep. The next day the pain finally subsided, and she was driven to the clinic for day two of the abortion procedure. The suctioning part of the abortion. On day two, she was put to sleep using general anesthesia. Needless to say, day two was a breeze for her and a nightmare for her unborn baby. When it was all over, she was given orange juice, crackers and told she did well during the procedure.

Jesus said, "For, behold, the darkness shall cover the earth, and gross darkness the people" (Isaiah 60:2).

My Question to God, Yeshua, and the Holy Spirit

Will my son (Christopher) still be a child or adult when I get to heaven?

Based on the following, I believe the answer is yes: he will still be a child waiting to run into my arms when I arrive in heaven.

1. The dew of Christ's youth. Jesus is in heaven with the dew of His youth. "Your people will offer themselves freely on the day of your power, in holy garments, from the womb of the morning, the dew

of your youth will be yours" (Psalm 110:3, ESV).

2. There is no pain or suffering in heaven; aging sometimes brings natural suffering and, eventually, leads to death. There is no death in heaven (only God's light and eternal life). So how can continued aging happen if Jesus has the dew of His youth in heaven?

The Woman Who Invented Planned Parenthood, M. Sanger

Only the first initial and the last name of the woman listed above will be included in this book. The full name of the person listed above is not worthy of being included in this book. However, there is a small notation I made while watching a documentary, which God sent to me while I was writing this book. Of all the horrible things that were revealed to me about the woman who invented abortion by creating Planned Parenthood, God revealed His thoughts of her to the world and myself in the most miraculous and subtle way. If you blink or don't pay attention, you will definitely miss it. See below.

M. Sanger

Born: September 14, 1879

Died: September 6, 1966

Numerology: 9/6/1966

Minor clarification of the number nine: all nines (one

meaning of the number nine in the Bible is "finality"). The Jewish day starts at sundown, but hours are counted from sunup, and it is thought that Jesus was crucified at 9:00 a.m., three hours after sunup (sunup being roughly at 6:00 a.m.).

Her death date contains the mark of the beast, three sixes, which represents absolute evil (see above), and the number nine, in some cases in the Bible, represents the destruction of evil or the evil one.

Translation: the total destruction of the evil one.

Interesting Parallels to the Number Nine in the Bible

^

Do numbers have meaning? Ask any physicist this question, and I believe the answer will be yes.

1. In the Old Testament, there were at least nine groups or individuals who practiced sorcery (evil).

2. The total destruction of Jerusalem's temple began in the Hebrew calendar on Ab 9 (destruction).

3. It was also the ninth day, Ab 9, that Herod's temple was burned to the ground by the Romans in AD 70 (evil).

4. Belshazzar called his astrologers and wise men to interpret the writing on the wall, which revealed that Belshazzar's kingdom and palace would be destroyed that night.

Literally, the story written below happened as this book was in the final stages of completion in 2021. The miracle story below revealed that God is still very near and present with me, guiding me through the process of completing this book.

A 2021 Miracle Day

This was not a dream; it was literally God's confirmation that this book and life *itself* are a supernatural miracle from God. By the year 2021, I was under the assumption that God had finished revealing all the hidden messages that I would need for this book. But God showed me otherwise.

My rendition of God's hidden message, miracle, revealed to me in 2021: "Nope, I'm with you all the way."

June 28, 2021

That day, while watching television, I turned to Daystar on channel 369. Daystar is one of my favorite religious channels. I was watching Joni Lamb as she was speaking to a male guest who was talking about a harrowing experience that he had with the police. He also spoke about his new book to inspire the world to come together. After watching this episode on Joni's show, I decided to go to the gym for a quick workout.

As I usually do, I left home and left the television

on because I didn't expect to be gone long and wanted to make sure I could use TVO to see any missed parts of the show. Upon my return home (approximately one hour later), the television was still on. Within a few minutes of being in the house, I just happened to hear the word "abortion" mentioned by a guest speaker. And as usual, whenever I heard someone speaking of abortion in any situation, I stopped to listen because abortion had become my life assignment. So, I stopped, turned toward the television, and began listening to see who was speaking and what they were saying about abortion. The guest speaker was a lady discussing abortion and her fight for life, which is also the title of her book about abortion. While initially listening to her speak, I had no idea of her name but, of course, continued to listen.

I began to admire her tenacity, strength, and vigor for defending the unborn, defenseless children in the womb. As I continued listening to her speak, the two female hosts who were interviewing her, while introducing her book to the audience, said her name, Lila Rose. Immediately after hearing her name, I didn't think much of it. However, within a few minutes, I begin thinking, *Where have I seen or heard this name before, Lila Rose?* Within a few minutes of contemplation, I stopped and stared at the television intensely, and suddenly my mouth dropped to the floor. I was experiencing an "aw" moment. I was in absolute disbelief about what was actually happening in real time, in 2021, while I was in the process of finalizing this book. So, I continued to sit with my eyes and ears glued to the television.

"I knew it. I knew it: that is it!" I exclaimed. The name Lily Rose was the name on one of the very special supernatural artifacts I found while walking somewhere in 2012. I believed (then and now) with all my heart that the card I found was sent to me by God, Yeshua, and the Holy Spirit. The picture on the card was a very special picture. It was a supernatural piece of artwork made 100 percent of multicolor rainbow glitter sprinkled on a light-brown background. I consider it priceless. The card was made by the hands of a child. I have never met the child who created the picture, and I can't exactly remember where or how I found it. I just remember finding it and feeling as though it was very special and somehow was sent to me for a reason, a hidden reason that may one day be revealed. I knew it was some sort of special message because I found it during the time that I was having all the supernatural dreams of my aborted son Christopher in heaven.

How likely is it that a picture I found in 2012 while walking somewhere (most likely in a school or park) had the same name inscribed on it (Lily Rose) as the name of the guest speaker (Lila Rose) on the Daystar television network, advocating for the lives of unborn children and vehemently fighting against abortion? Can someone say, "Wow"?

The photo (above) is a black-and-white photo, so it's hard to see the intricate details, so let me explain what you probably cannot see. To see this picture in color, visit our Instagram page: @godsanswertoabortion.

The Angel Is in the Details

1. The background paper is light brown, like the color of the earth or dry dirt.
2. The image in the center is the purple (lavender) color, the color of royalty.
3. On the right side of the image is a tiny x.
4. On the left side of the image is a tiny heart.
5. The primary color of the image is light purple or lavender, and there are sprinkles of other glittering colors.

6. The image (if you look closely) resembles the shape of a tiny child's face with a tiny neck. The tiny x and tiny heart are the eyes.

7. There appears to be the shape of an ear on the right side (the picture is like someone looking at you).

8. And finally, look closely at the top of the image: there appears to be an arm holding a long object pointing upward toward the sky. It reminds me of my dream of the angel made of clouds, blowing the horn that was pointed upward toward the heavens. I am sure the child responsible for creating this beautiful masterpiece was not aware that they were creating a supernatural prophetic work of art for God, but God was.

And if everything I said earlier about the guest speaker's name supernaturally being inscribed on the photo of the child's face I found in 2012 wasn't enough, do you remember what I said about leaving home to go to the gym and leaving my television turned on channel 369? When I returned home, as I continued to sit listening to the female speaker, I suddenly noticed that my television was no longer on the channel that I had left it on. It was now on channel 373, the Word Network channel. I know for certain I didn't leave my television on this channel because I rarely turn to channel 373, not out of choice but more out of habit. Again, I sat scratching my head, wondering who had turned my television while I was at the gym. So, immediately I ran into the man cave and asked my boyfriend if he had changed the channel from 369 to 373 on my television, and of course, he replied no. The guest speaker was actually not speaking on the Daystar Channel; she was speaking on the Word Network channel; thus, had my television not somehow supernaturally ended up on the Word Network channel, I would have never encountered the guest speaker Lila Rose talking about her book, *Fighting for Life*. This was a true miracle.

I discovered the card made of rainbow-colored glitter with the name Lily Rose inscribed on it in 2012. I discovered the female crusader fighting for the lives of unborn children, Lila Rose, in 2021. She became a voice fighting for babies who have no choice, no voice, and are utterly defenseless victims in their mothers' wombs.

She understood and answered God's assignment; I can't wait to meet her one day soon.

Jesus said, "I would thou wert cold or hot. So then because thou art lukewarm, and neither cold nor hot, I will spue thee out of my mouth" (Revelation 3:15–16).

When it comes to abortion, don't be a fence-sitter.

You must choose.

Peter, a disciple of Yeshua, while on a journey to a city, became hungry and wanted something to eat. While the men were preparing the meat for him, he fell into a trance and saw the heavens open. Paraphrasing: there came a voice to him, saying, "Rise, Peter, kill and eat." But Peter replied, "By no means, Lord, for I have never eaten anything that is common or unclean." And the voice came to him again a second time, "What God has made clean do not call common" (Acts 10:9–48).

Hence, what God has chosen for us (if that is to become pregnant), who are we to reject since it is God's choice?

God's choice is always the right choice for our lives, it may not seem like it at first or in the moment during what appears to be an imperfect storm (accidental or unplanned pregnancy), but somehow, in the end, all things work together for our good, even if it is painful.

The other side of the coin is (if you choose to believe your pregnancy was not God's will), there is also a place in the Bible that discusses the principles of the law, which suggests that every cause has a natural effect. This is the law. Thus, unprotected sex outside of the will of God will sometimes result in a natural consequence (an unwanted pregnancy). Every man has free will.

"Be not deceived; God is not mocked: for whatsoever a man soweth, that shall he also reap" (Galatians 6:7).

PS

I have found that if only I had followed the suggestions made by God in the Bible, I would have avoided so many mistakes and pitfalls that almost always lead to despair, misery, sadness, and poor choices.

Chapter 18

My Dream of Heaven

Although this was only a dream, it was so vivid and felt so real it felt like I actually took a trip to heaven. I have shortened the dream to speak specifically about the parts that felt most like heaven to me. The dream started with me riding on a bus with my dad's ex-wife Pat, a few friends, and a mysterious man whose identity was never revealed in the dream.

We decided to go eat or make lunch, and somehow, we ended up at a table filled with food. I made a sandwich to eat, but I didn't like the sandwich that I had made for myself. The mysterious man had also made a sandwich for himself. I was able to eat a small bit of his sandwich. I liked the sandwich the mysterious man had made for himself, so I wanted to eat his instead of mine. However, I knew it would be selfish for me to eat his entire sandwich. I guess he gathered that I liked his sandwich more than I liked mine. He advised me to get some bread and toast it because it would make my sandwich taste much better. So, I toasted my bread and sat down to eat. After eating my sandwich, I wanted to call Mr. N. so that I could find him because I suddenly realized that he had not called me all day and it was past four o'clock p.m. I am not sure if I ever made that call.

In another scene of the dream, Pat, my dad's ex-wife, a few of my friends (identities unknown), and I all got into a bus, which turned out to be a party bus because we were headed to a Halloween party. We sat in the back of the bus. Pat sat to my left, and there were several other people sitting around us (identities unknown). We were all talking about the homes we wanted to live in, and we were talking about Pat's home. Initially, I was jealous of Pat's home, and we all spoke very negatively about her home. After a short time, Pat began to agree with us, and she began thinking that she needed a better home than the one she had. But before she yielded to our ideas, I admitted the truth to her and told her that she had chosen well. Her home was a beautiful home, nestled in a beautiful community. And it was not just a regular to-do home at all; it was a huge mansion. Pat's house is the first house we encountered as we entered the community.

And suddenly we looked outside the windows of the bus and saw the outside was filled with beautiful clouds in the sky. We were suddenly in a city of vintage-looking mansions, some of which were far off in the distance. Suddenly, we were all off the bus, sitting in this colorful place with children playing. There were children of all ethnic backgrounds. And suddenly, when I looked to my right, I noticed two men passing by us. They were riding on something that looked like a carriage with a donkey attached to the front. They were sitting just behind the donkey with straps attached to it. There was a carriage pulled behind them. There appeared to be food in the wooden carriage. The mystery food or fruit was mostly unseen, but I could see the top of the food, which was revealed through the upper part of the bags. The food was beautiful in color. The color was like an illuminated turquoise, super-bright turquoise, and definitely a color that I had never seen before.

The men were driving up what appeared to be a long meandering road leading up a mountain surrounded by beautiful clouds. There was a huge castle far off in the distance, nestled in the clouds at the top of the mountain. The two men guiding the wooden carriage driven by a donkey appeared to be of Latino or Middle Eastern descent. There was a dark child coming down that same mountain while playing (ethnicity unknown). There were red flower bunches to my right, which appeared to be a bed of bright-red blooming roses with the most beautiful red I had ever seen. There were tropical colors everywhere, more tropical than in Hawaii. There were children playing everywhere, and strangely enough, they did not see us looking at them.

Suddenly, I saw a huge grizzly bear walking down a small hill toward a child, a little Asian boy playing with a ball. I became frantic and started telling everyone, "Look, we need to save him." So, I jumped up as if to try to run and help him, but my fear of the bear caused me to turn around and run away. I ran to the left. But when I looked back, the grizzly bear had walked right past the child and did not harm him. Then I heard a voice say, "Look, there's a coyote or dog on another grassy mountain." But then we noticed that the coyotes or dogs were walking among all the children but not harming them. They (the wild animals) were not dangerous. I remember thinking, *Wow, this place is absolutely beautiful*. There were tall red-oak trees everywhere and beautiful roads leading in different directions. There were grassy fields with shiny green grass. The color was a beautiful green that I had never seen before. There were bright white clouds and luminous colors everywhere. There were beautifully carved mansions that appeared off in the distance, all joined together, made of clouds but white-grayish in color. And suddenly, I awoke.

When I awoke, the man on television, Daystar, said these words: "God said, 'Go to your brother and make peace with your brother. Leave your prayer and, after you have forgiven your brother, return to Me, and I will forgive you.'" True-story, real-life television.

The Morning after the Dream in Heaven

The next morning, after awakening from my beautiful dream of heaven, I became curious and decided to call

Pat, my dad's ex-wife and the mother of my sister. My sister and I had previously fallen out and had not spoken for several years. I asked Pat one question: Was she house shopping? She replied yes. The irony is that in real life, Pat and I never got along, and we never liked each other. Thus, this was no easy call to make. Sometime later, I spoke to my sister as well. We have forgiven each other but remain distant.

Prophetic Dream of Hell Number One

I was walking down a long corridor with walls made of windows where I could see outside. The floor was gray in color, and there were women walking in front of me. They were all tall, beautiful women who appeared to be models. They were headed to Las Vegas for a modeling contest. They were all walking in front of me, so they made it to the taxi before I did. The taxi was gray in color as well, but it was not a car; it was a taxi van, similar to that of a party van. I thought they would drive off without me because I was walking slower and lagging behind them, but no, they waited.

Last night, I dreamed of demons attacking me again. A female demon dressed in an all-black neoprene mesh workout suit was stomping me with her feet. The attacks of the demons were always unprovoked and always continuous.

October 8, 2013

After the final dream of my son Christopher in Hawaii, I started having dreams of hell and demons. I experienced several dreams of demons attacking me and at least four dreams of hell. I have not included all the dreams of hell in this book for the purposes of keeping the book shorter in length; however, I included a few for context and revelation. I would be remiss if I had only shared the beautiful dreams of heaven and not the other side, known as hell.

Fact: in the Bible, Jesus Spoke of Hell More than of Heaven

Thus, I thought it absolutely necessary to share with you the dreams that I had of hell. There had to be a reason the Holy Spirit allowed me to experience these dreams as well.

All is intended or is a result of sin.

So why do innocent people die?

Sometimes the sin isn't related to the innocent victim but is the result of the sinner committing the sin. But remember: it is not God who brings about destruction and death. It is the evil one.

"The thief comes only to steal and kill and destroy. I have come that they may have life and have it more abundantly" (John 10:10, ESV).

266

God takes no pleasure in the death of anyone, innocent or wicked. He wishes that all would repent of their sins and live.

"For I take no pleasure in the death of anyone, declares the Sovereign LORD. Repent and live!" (Ezekiel 18:32, NIV).

"Repent" means: turn away from your life of sin and walk on a new path; it is more than just confessing the Lord as your Lord and Savior. We must walk in the light, live in the light, and love in the light that we might live eternally.

Prophetic Dream of Hell Number Two

Demons were attacking me again. I saw a very long staircase that led straight down into the center of the earth. The stairs were so deep they appeared infinite. They were made of dark gray or black hard iron and brass. There was a figure heading downward on the stairs. The figure was that of a human being, and it was completely hairless from head to toe. Its skin was darker than the night sky, a true black, like tar. It looked dirty, dusty, and dingy as if it had blotches of mud and dark patches of dirt all over it. I could not tell whether it was male or female; it had no masculine or feminine gender identity. But for some reason, I took it to be male, maybe out of the habit of how my human brain has been trained.

Somehow, I ended up walking up a staircase instead of getting down the staircase. The body of the being, demon, or thing lay still, without movement, at the top of the black staircase. It lay there completely motionless. It, whatever it was, appeared dead and without life. Then suddenly, it began to arise: slowly, very slowly. Its movement appeared similar to the way Hollywood movies depict vampires arising from their caskets. It rose slowly and sat straight up. It turned and looked at me and began approaching me. I ran until I could no longer see the demon. But at every corner I turned, the demon changed appearance and was still there. It remained behind me, following me; every corner I turned, it was there. Every time I thought I had lost it or outran it, it would reappear in a different form and location. I saw it (the hairless demon) getting out of cars, walking out of the buildings; no matter where I turned, it was still there, reappearing in different forms and places.

The Woman Who Was Never Afraid to Speak of Hell

One thing I have noticed: I rarely hear anyone speak of hell, and doing so makes people shun you or cast you into the doom-and-gloom crowd. But is it not true that Jesus spoke more of hell than of heaven in the Bible? Why do you think He did this?

It is a well-accepted fact that Jesus spoke more of hell than He did of heaven.

Mother Angelica from the EWTN channel often refer-
enced hell and was unafraid to tell a person that if they did
not repent (turn away from a life of sin and follow Christ),
they were going to end up in a place they would deeply
regret getting (hell).

Jesus speaks the following about hell: hell is a place of
eternal torment (Luke 16:23); of unquenchable fire (Mark
9:48); where the worm dies not (Mark 9:48); where people will gnash their teeth in anguish and regret (Matthew
13:42), and from which there is no return, even to warn
loved ones (Luke 16:19–31). He calls hell a place of "outer
darkness" (Matthew 25:30).

Prophetic Dream of the End Times

October 4, 2013

I felt like I was being escorted by a guide whom I could
not see. I could feel his/her presence there with me, guiding me, but they remained hidden. We were in a part of the
sea, a part that I had never seen in real life before. We were
literally floating on top of the sea, but I wouldn't really
call it floating; it felt more as if we were flying or glid-
ing just above the water but moving at the speed of light.
The sea was dark, and the clouds were dark. The clouds
and the sea seemed to connect as if they were one. The
clouds seemed to hover just above the sea, like no more

than a few feet above the water. The water and the clouds moved with speed and intensity. My guide and I were flying with the clouds and the sea, also moving at the same speed. We were moving just above the clouds and the sea as if we were one with the sea and clouds. However, I noticed I could not see beyond a few feet in front of me. The clouds were so thick the open sea was hidden behind them. I could only see the water under me and approximately ten or fifteen feet in front of me.

All I remember about this dream is that I was somewhere out in the deep ocean, a deep part of the sea that had never been seen by natural man. The sky was black, but not black like a night sky, rather gloomy dark grayish-black combined. Definitely not a pretty sight. Then suddenly, I was taken to another scene in the same dream. In the second part of the dream, I was in a country that appeared to be in the Middle East. We (my guide and I) were riding in an off-road vehicle that felt like a jeep, but I could not see the vehicle that we were in. The terrain on which we traveled was very rocky and bumpy. The region of the world where we were was very, very hot. I had the air conditioning on full blast because I could not stand the heat. My guide warned me that if I continued running the air conditioning so high, we might run out of gas, and that would be it for us. In other words, deadly. I still don't understand why, but that was the feeling I got. While riding, I could see people on the sides of the road. They were walking with camels and appeared busy as though they were going about their daily lives and activities as usual. They did not see us at all, but I got the feeling that if we ran out of gas, they might be able to detect and/or see us.

What I know for sure is we were moving at a superfast speed, so fast, it was as if we were moving at the speed of light or maybe faster. Most importantly, I remember the ride and terrain were very rigid, bumpy, and uncomfortable, and suddenly, the dream was over.

PS

I have never traveled outside of the United States, except for going to Mexico. I have jokingly referred to myself as geographically challenged. Thus, I have no idea of what the Middle East is like, but the dream took me to a place I had never been, a hot place with camels and large land areas that might have been covered with sand.

The Mystery of the Year 2013 Revealed

When I began analyzing the year 2013, hindsight proved to be a twenty-twenty vision. When looking at several prophetic events that occurred in 2013, I came to believe that God's prophetic revelations of things to come, including death, destruction, and the curse being released on the earth, began unfolding in 2013.

For whatever reason, the number thirteen has a deep

history of being a number associated with fear, evil, death, and destruction. The mystery of this number is still unknown to me. However, during my supernatural dreams, visions, mysterious sightings, finding supernatural artifacts, signs, and wonders, I also received a subtle revelation about the year 2013. I was shown through several terrible real-life events that the year 2013 was the prophetic year of the release of death and destruction on the earth and what I believe may be the release of the-en-of-times curse onto the earth. Hence the year of the beginning of the end might have arrived. And if your end was eminent, signs of death came upon you (death knocked at your door) in 2013. That doesn't mean 2013 is the year a person would die, but it means that death might have come to you in one way or another, hidden and unknown to its intended target.

The thirteenth constellation: it is a widely accepted idea that there is a thirteenth unseen constellation or Zodiac sign, *Ophiuchus*; the thirteenth sign is known to some or thought to be "the serpent bearer."

February 2013: an asteroid mysteriously strikes Russia by flying over Russia at a very close range. It could be seen moving faster than the speed of light. The asteroid was not detected by scientists prior to its descent from the universe to the earth, which goes to show you science is not bigger than God.

April 2013: NASA detected what they referred to as a

monstrous gamma-ray burst huddling through space at the speed of light. The gamma ray was extremely close to the earth and was closer to the earth than anyone had ever seen before. Again, science was not expecting this event.

The year 2013: Bob Jones' interview on God TV.

Bob Jones, who is sometimes referred to as a prophet, indicated during his interview the year 2013 was the year of the beginning of the awakening to the "eternal harvest" to come.

Eternal Harvest

Concerning all human beings, there are two types of biblical harvests: one harvest that leads to paradise and heavenly awakenings and one that leads to death, hell, and destruction. Your harvest is determined not only by the seeds you plant but also by the seeds you feed.

Bob and his interviewer cited the following Bible verses: "For, behold, the darkness shall cover the earth, and gross darkness the people: but the LORD shall arise upon thee, and his glory shall be seen upon thee" (Isaiah 60:2).

"That in the ages to come, He might shew the exceeding riches of his grace in his kindness toward us" (Ephesians 2:7).

The year 2013: a famous rapper who shall remain nameless was descended upon by the curse of death through a woman (unbeknownst to her). The rapper was sent a sign (whisper from the Holy Spirit), but no one saw it. Once, the rapper was asked by a famous radio host when and how he was introduced to the healer, a healer he had become fond of. The rapper replied, "My girl." This rapper would die six years later.

The number six in the Torah represents man, beast, flesh, work, sacrifice, intimacy, knowledge, sacrificial love but is most commonly held as the number of the anti-Christ, the beast, and judgment. The Torah suggests the number thirteen will have some of the same properties as the number six, and some of the negative attributes of the number thirteen are apathy, indifference, and fear. But the Torah also notes that the number thirteen can also mean love if it is in union with and represents God.

February 2013: Pope Benedict XVI was the first pope to resign in 600 years. On the night of the crowning of the new pope, Pope Francis, lightning struck the Vatican twice. Pope Francis was predicted to be the last pope by a famous astrologer who predicted the end of the world to occur during the time of the last pope.

October 13, 2013: the death of my mother was completely unexpected and due to an accidental fall she had while walking in her garden. Death tried to stop the writing of this book by crushing my heart, but the Holy Spirit did not let me stay in the muddy waters. God's hand lifted me out of one of the darkest periods of my life.

The March of the Blind

October 03, 2021

It was the day of the annual Women's March that promotes and fosters support for the pro-choice movement, hence a women's right to choose. The participants and supporters of this march call it "the women's march." I call it "the march of the blind."

On the day of the march, a news reporter interviewed a mother who was participating in the march with her three children. The news reporter asked the woman why she had chosen to attend the march, and she replied, "I am here because I want my children to know the right thing to do in life."

I sat there looking at the television, puzzled. "The right thing to do?" What is the right thing to do? Teach our children that it is okay to murder babies in our wombs if we choose to because we feel like they were a mistake?

Chapter 19

So, What Is God's Answer to Abortion?

The following answers were revealed to me in dreams, supernatural experiences, visions, mysteries, wonders, numbers, and biblical parables.

God's Answer Is...

Life, the human soul, is given by *God*. Therefore, the giving and taking of life is not man's choice. It is God's choice in *all* circumstances.

Our bodily temple, hence the place that houses our soul, is made of stardust. Both babies born into the physical realm and babies who were born into the realm where God resides in heaven are loved by God and have a very special part of His great and beautiful universe.

We are *all* living stars.

A Little-Known Fact

The human-body composition shares many (if not all)

of the same elemental compounds of which stars are made.

Jesus said to the mothers and fathers who abort (murder) their unborn children in the womb (myself included), "I present before you *life* and *death*; *choose life*" (Deuteronomy 30:15, paraphrased).

To those who are pro-choice or supporters of abortion, indifferent, or undecided, Jesus said, "I wish that you were hot or cold, for I will spit the lukewarm out of my mouth" (Revelation 3:15–16, paraphrased).

To staunch abortion advocates and doctors of murder, Jesus said, "Behold, all souls are mine; as the soul of the father, so also the soul of the son is mine; the soul that sinneth, it shall die" (Ezekiel 18:4).

To the mothers who are victims of rape or incest:

1. My heart truly goes out to you, as I have also been a victim of this terrible crime.

2. Follow God's Word. Always listen to God. Don't trust in yourself; trust in God and His plan for your life. He will never fail you.

3. Please try to conceptualize that the child is just as much a victim as you are. God says *never ever* should anyone die for the sins of someone else.

4. Why should the baby's life be taken away for the sins of their fathers and/or mothers?

Jesus says, "The soul that sinneth, it shall die. The son shall not bear the iniquity of the father, neither shall the father bear the iniquity of the son: the righteousness of the righteous shall be upon him, and the wickedness of the wicked shall be upon him" (Ezekiel 18:20).

To the mothers who are victims of rape or incest or an unwanted pregnancy:

God will hear your cries, sorrows, and prayers. He will award you for your bravery, sacrifice, and reverence.

You can overcome being the victim; you are the righteousness of God in Jesus Christ; you are the apple of His eye; you are not a victim; you are a victorious human being; you are a child of God, and you will win in the end if you faint not!

Jesus said, "But they that wait on the Lord shall renew their strength, they shall mount up with wings as eagles, they shall run and not be weary, and they shall walk and not faint" (Isaiah 40:31).

Rabbi Manis Friedman once told a story of two men engaged in a physical battle that led to the injury of a woman who was pregnant. He described how the woman and child were injured, but the child's life was not lost. However, even if the child and mother were injured, the child must still be allowed to live; hence it must be given flesh. In a YouTube video "Love, Love, Love, Love, Love, What Is Love?" Rabbi Manis Friedman says, "But if there is a catastrophe, let it be given a flesh, for a flesh let it be given to her" (2018).

Hence the mother is to allow the baby to be born. The perpetrator of the catastrophe will be judged accordingly by God for his sin. But if the mother and the rapist or incestuous person cause injury to the child, they will both be liable for the sin.

To those who have had an abortion and are struggling to forgive themselves, Jesus said,

"For a righteous man may fall seven times and rise again, But the wicked shall fall by calamity" (Proverbs 24:16, NKJV).

If you have been knocked down by this situation, get up, wipe your tears, ask God for forgiveness, repent, and keep moving forward.

"The righteousness of the righteous [man] will be credited to him, and the wickedness of the wicked will be charged against him" (Ezekiel 18:20, NIV).

Life is beautiful and must be lived fully, so forgive yourself: you have a beautiful child in heaven who loves you still.

To you who are sometimes for abortion and sometimes against abortion, depending on the circumstances of the mother's pregnancy (i.e., rape or incest), Jesus said, "I know thy works, that thou art neither cold nor hot. I would thou wert cold or hot. So then because thou art lukewarm, and neither cold nor hot, I will spue thee out of my mouth" (Revelation 3:15–16).

Notice: the words spoken by Yeshua, Jesus, in the above passage are included in Revelation, the last book in the Bible, which is largely known to speak of the end of days known to man on the earth. Ponder why the above words spoken by Jesus are included in the book of Revelation. It is my belief that the words spoken are also a parable with a hidden message, meaning that one must choose life or death, and one is encouraged to do this before the end of days.

To Christians, i.e., persons who profess to be believers in Christ and are sometimes for abortion and sometimes against abortion, depending on the circumstances of the mother's pregnancy (i.e., rape or incest), and Christians who believe in a woman's right to choose (to murder her baby in the womb) but profess to be Catholics, Baptists... etc.:

"This people draweth nigh unto me with their mouth, and honoureth me with their lips, but their heart is far from me" (Matthew 15:8).

To the judges and lawmakers who support a woman's right to choose: "But in vain they do worship me, teaching for doctrines the commandments of men" (Matthew 15:9).

My Question to You

I recently posed this same question to a friend: Can a person be in heaven and hell at the same time, in any circumstance?

There's only one answer: *no.*

Can a person be for abortion and against abortion, for

murder and against murder?

Yes.

Can a person be for the murder of babies in any circumstance and still go to heaven?

The answer is...*no.*

You are either for abortion or against abortion. Period.

One must choose. Of those voices that scream and shout, "My body, my choice," I ask, then why not legalize prostitution? It is your body, so shouldn't it be your choice in this circumstance as well? So, why can't you sell it for a profit if you choose to?

Why should it be okay for a man to tell you what to do with your body in this circumstance? Oh, yeah, because prostitution is morally wrong?

Okay, is taking a baby's life in the womb (murder of a baby) morally wrong?

So, what is abortion in the first place? Is the word "abortion" not merely coded language for "murder"?

Is it not just a word that lessens the impact of the pain of its true meaning?

Let's be honest: abortion and murder are synonyms.

Is not the end result for both words the same? A life goes from this earth; a living soul dies; a living soul ceases to exist in this dominion.

Planned parenting (parenthood) is planned life or death

for babies in the womb, with the choice being taken away from God and placed in the hands of mothers and fathers in accordance with man's law and not God's will.

My prayer for you is that you hear and see the truth and not be offended, that you know the true will of God and walk in the light.

Jesus said, "Ask, and it shall be given to you; seek, and ye shall find" (Matthew 7:7).

Just ask Him, and He will forgive you just like He forgave me.

Seek the truth, and you will find it. Seek the truth, and it will make you free.

Seek the truth and let it guide you to a beautiful eternity, paradise, where your beautiful child awaits you.

Christine Caine

This is a woman who has a televised ministry on some of the most popular religious stations. She, for all accounts, is a very successful woman who has risen above what I would call average. She openly reveals her journey and not-so-flattering start to life. She was born to unknown parents. She does not know anything about her biological parents (mother or father). She does not know if she was an orphan at birth, a child who was conceived as a result of a rape, or if she was left abandoned somewhere. But what she does know is that none of the above stopped her from becoming a great human being. So, was her life worth living?

We never know what could become of a child, regardless of how their life started. It is not how we start; it is always how we choose to finish.

Who is more guilty of murder?

The person who signs the death warrant and orders the execution or the person who pulls the switch to release the lethal electricity into the person's body?

Dear God, Yeshua, and the Holy Spirit

I hope with the deepest sincerity of my heart that this book will shine a light for those living in darkness, open the eyes of those who cannot see, and open the doors to heaven's revelation for all to hear and see what You revealed to me about abortion.

Jesus, You said, "Can the blind lead the blind? Shall they not both fall into a ditch?" (Luke 6:39).

Conversation with My Cousin

While speaking to my cousin, I asked, "Are you a Christian?"

He replied, "Yes."

I continued, "What do you think about abortion?"

He replied emphatically, "It is absolutely the woman's choice; it is her body; she should have a right to do what she wants with her own body." He continued, "I am taking spirituality out of it; this is about a woman and her right to choose what she wants to do with her own body."

"Cousin, you can never separate the spirit of God from any issue that involves life or our lives. That is where most human beings go wrong; they try to categorize sin and certain situations to isolate sin from God. You can never separate God from the equation. The very breath that you breathe is from God; the blood flowing in your veins is God. God must not be excluded from any part of our lives; to do so is to invite death in."

He replied, "Well, I am just saying I support the woman's right to choose."

"To choose what?"

He responded, "She should have a right to choose."

I asked him, "To choose what?"

"What she wants to do with her body."

I responded, "Finish the sentence."

He replied, "What?" sounding a bit puzzled.

I said, "Finish the entire sentence. Here is what you are really saying when you say you believe a woman should have the right to choose to do what she wants to do with her body. If you complete the entire sentence, it will sound something like this: 'I believe a woman should have a right to choose to do what she wants to do with her body, and if she chooses to have an abortion (kill her unborn baby), she should be able to do so because it is her body; it is her choice.'

"Thus, you are supporting the woman's right to murder her own child if she so chooses. Cousin, you must complete the sentence if you are being honest with yourself regarding what it is that you are really supporting. You are not just supporting the woman's right to choose; you are supporting the woman's right to choose to end the life of her unborn child."

Be aware (beware) of what you are supporting.

The Two Thieves on the Cross

+++

The story goes that while both men (the two thieves) were hanging next to Jesus on the cross, suffering the same gruesome fate as Jesus, both responded to Jesus's crucifixion very differently. The thief on the right, who came to be known as the good thief, rebuked the bad thief, saying,

> Dost not thou fear God, seeing thou art in the same condemnation? And we are indeed justly; for we receive the due reward of our deeds: but this man hath done nothing amiss. And he [the good thief] said unto Jesus, Lord, remember me when thou comest into thy

kingdom. And Jesus said unto him, Verily I
say unto thee, today shalt thou be with me in
paradise.

Luke 23:40–42

The bad thief on the left says to Jesus, "Are you not the
Messiah? Save Yourself and us" (Luke 23:39, paraphrased).
He echoed the same voice as the crowd, thus committing
the same sin or crime as the crowd: the crucifixion of Yeshua. He did this with his words while hanging on a cross
next to Jesus. He didn't nail Jesus to the cross, and for all
intents and purposes, we know that he wasn't walking and
chanting with the crowd and the Pharisees and Sadducees in
the streets because presumably, he was hanging on a cross.
Nevertheless, the Bible seems to indicate that he would suffer the same fate as those who supported and ordered the
death of Yeshua, our Lord and Savior. The good thief, on
the other hand, confessed Jesus as the Lord, repented of his
sins, and asked to be saved. And he did this with his words;
thus, Jesus said that day he would be with Him in paradise.

Do not think that any word uttered from our mouths
does not carry significant meaning to God, Yeshua, and the
Holy Spirit.

The Bible says, "Death and life are in the power of the
tongue, and those who love it, will eat its fruit" (Proverbs
18:21, NKJV).

Yeshua said,

But I say unto you, That every idle word that men shall speak, they shall give account thereof in the day of judgement. For by thy words thou shalt be justified, and by thy words, thou shalt be condemned.

Matthew 12:36–37

Question:

What are you saying about abortion?

Trivia question:

How are abortion, the Holocaust, and slavery alike? Can abortion be compared to the Holocaust? Can abortion be compared to slavery? Yes, I know your first answer is likely going to be "Absolutely not." Some might even find the suggestion offensive.

But wait before you answer or judge the question.

Listen, Look, and See

In each of these cases, someone dies. Yes or no? In

each of these cases, the atrocities that are being committed against human life are justified by the ruling class and persons involved in committing the injustices against those (often innocent victims) who were given no voice and who had no choice. Is this not true in each of those cases: abortion, slavery, and the Holocaust? If you're being honest, there's only one answer: yes.

There is one other way they are alike...
One word sums up the answer:
"Dehumanization."

In each of the above travesties (abortion, the holocaust, and slavery), the human being is not seen as a human being at all. He or she is not seen as a human being needing to be loved, celebrated, and protected. In each of the above, he or she is seen as either not worthy of life and existence at all (aborted babies), existing as a mere nuisance that needs annihilation (the Jews), or existing as a mere animal to be bought and sold like cattle (the slave).

How easy would it be for a mother or father to allow an innocent life (their own unborn child, embryo, in the womb) to be murdered by vacuum suctioning, hence a complete crushing of the body, if they deemed the living cells and heartbeat in some cases and a fully forming baby in other cases as a human being?

The word "abortion" dehumanizes the baby (medical term "embryo"), making the baby, a living soul in the mother's womb, no more than a surgical procedure to be completed, hence, a mere mission to be executed.

How easy would it have been for the Nazis to murder millions of innocent Jews (mothers, fathers, sons, daughters, grandparents, etc.) if they could have heard the voice of God, saying, "These are My children too, and their lives are just as valuable as yours?"

How easy would it have been for the slave traders to stockpile, murder, beat, kill, and enslave millions of innocent Africans if they could have heard the voice of God, saying, "These are My children too, and their lives are just as valuable as yours?"

On the last note, as I was writing this interesting parallel, God revealed another hidden truth and parallel about life to me.

God, Yeshua, and the Holy Spirit visited me in a dream and presented the following parallel: When a man dies, when does his soul leave his body?

God's answer, as revealed to me: "Immediately."

When a baby is conceived in the mother's womb (sperm cell enters the egg), when does the soul enter the cells of the embryo?

God's answer as revealed to me: "Immediately."

Interestingly, God's answer did not come in the form of a numeric value (seconds, minutes, days, weeks, months). His answer came in the form of a word. Hence, the number cannot be calculated in terms of quantity as we humans calculate when life begins. God's word is life.

Parallelisms in the Bible

Note: this message was sent to me supernaturally. The excerpt of parallelisms highlighted in the Bible is from the book of Isaiah, chapter one. The presentation was provided by a LoveIsrael.org YouTube video presentation.

This prophecy was given to me by way of the LoveIsrael.org YouTube channel, where a Bible story was told, a story that was written about the Israelites as a prophetic message telling how the Israelites violated God. The story of the Israelites is for all men to hear so they can learn and be warned.

Israelites had moved away from God, were a nation that sinned, that was very heavy in their sins. Israel did not know God and was not paying attention, not studying, and not giving enough attention to God. Basically, God was not pleased with the people, and therefore, there was going to be a negative outcome. The people had violated everything, the laws of God and the laws of man.

The ox and donkey are described as knowing who their owners are. They recognize and know their owners over themselves. But Israel did not know who their Lord was. God's people did not know God and were not paying attention. Isaiah pointed out how God was not important to the people, and because of this, God was not pleased with the people. Therefore, there was going to be an outcome from God's negative disposition about the people (Israel), a people (nation) heavy in their inequities. They had violated the Word of God in a very serious manner; they were offspring of evildoers; they were sons or children that were corrupt, and they had left the Lord. Through their choice of sin, inequity, and transgressions, the nation had left God. They spoke incorrectly and in an improper way against the Lord, and they turned backward.

Noted Parallelisms Made in Isaiah's Prophecy to the Israelites

I believe Israel in this Bible story can be compared to the modern United States.

Story of the Israelites and the United States

The head and the heart are synonymous with thinking, a thought process. So, Israel, in two ways, with their mind and with their heart, were making poor decisions. They had a sick way of thinking, and their thought processes were not pleasing to God. And there was nothing being done to bring health or healing to the children of Israel (nation).

The Heavens and the Earth. The Ox and the Donkey

The fact that Israel did not know and did not pay attention led to them making poor decisions, corruption, evildoings, and leaving the Lord.

The spiritual condition of the people and the physical condition of the land: their land was desolate, their cities burned with fire, the land before them was filled with foreigners, and they devoured it.

Hence, the nation that turned away from the Lord was being attacked and overtaken by foreigners. Like a city that is being laid siege. This nation was compared to Sodom and Gomorrah.

As a nation (United States), have we turned away from the Lord by allowing babies to continue to be murdered in their mothers' wombs? Do you believe God, Yeshua, and the Holy Spirit are pleased with babies being murdered in their mothers' wombs?

Has anyone noticed the recent events with inclement weather, fires, disasters, increased murder and violence, racial hatred, multi variants of COVID-19 that won't go away and let the world get back to normal?

To the Mothers and Fathers of Aborted Children

Jesus said, "For we walk by faith, not by sight" (2 Corinthians 5:7).

Many of you have not seen your children in heaven, but trust me when I say they are there waiting for you. They want to meet you, and they truly love you. All they know is love, not hate, and for them, there was never a goodbye. All they have ever known is love because they were born in heaven, and all there is in heaven is love, light, and laughter.

Letter to My Son

Dear Son Christopher,

I can hardly write these words without crying. I truly want to apologize to you for what I did to you and for not protecting, loving, and cherishing you the way that I should have. Please forgive me, for I know not what I do. I was foolish, and I was a fool. In that moment that I allowed you to be hurt (brutally crushed by a doctor), I knew not what I was doing. I did not understand life according to God's will; I only understood life according to man and his laws and rules. God had to show me the truth because I had been lied to. God opened my eyes so that I could see the petty follies that I commit.

And today, the irony is, Son, I would gladly give my life for you in any circumstance so that you might have the chance to live. I would gladly change places with you so that you might have a chance to know life as I have known it. And although I am not happy with this world and truly

294

would not want to bring a child into it, I now know that it is not my choice to choose life or death for any living soul. That choice belongs to God and God alone.

I know in my heart of hearts that if given a choice, you would have chosen life for yourself. You would have chosen to live. And why not? Because isn't life beautiful, no matter the circumstance, if you know Jesus? With every fiber of my body, mind, and soul, I hope that I can see you again. That I can see your face again, your smile again, and that we will meet in heaven again.

And although I do not deserve your love at all, you gave me your love anyway, and for that, I am truly grateful and forever thankful to my God (Yahweh), Yeshua, and the Holy Spirit. Thank You, Jesus, for Your saving grace.

My Letter to Jesus

Jesus,

You found me in a garbage can and lifted me out. To most, I was nothing more than garbage, a one-night thing to be thrown out.

To You, I was everything: I was valuable; I was love, and I was light.

You found me lost on a crooked, winding, narrow road and shined a light for me to see. I was lost, and You became my guide.

I was hatted because of my darker skin tone, and You

loved me and convinced me that I was the apple of Your eye.

I was valueless to most, and You came to me on a dark, winding, narrow road to hell and spoke these words to me: "Let Me treasure you."

Ladies and gentlemen, I assure you that there is no love like the love of God, *agape love.*

God, thank You for Your love, forgiveness, mercy, and grace!

And most of all, thank You for my life!

In Yeshua's name, I pray this prayer, amen.

Dear reader,

Take a moment to ponder this:

If you have had an abortion and can fathom the idea that you have a child waiting for you in heaven, use the space below to write three things you would say to your child now.

1.

2.

3.

This is not the end but rather the beginning for you.

He or she who listeneth shall repenteth, taketh courage, trusteth God, and goeth!

Bonus Prophetic Dream

I have never claimed to have the gift of foresight, but this dream seemed to be sent to me by God to foretell a tragic event soon to come.

Prophetic Dream of Nipsey Hussle, Tha Great

This dream came eleven days before his death.

Please note that I was not going to include this dream in this book because it didn't seem to fit with the content of this book, its prophetic message. However, I am a true believer in the Holy Spirit and the ability of the Holy Spirit to communicate with us. Thus, in like manner, the nudge of the Holy Spirit continued without ceasing when I came to the conclusion that I must write this book about my aborted son in heaven. After Nipsey Hussle's death (a person whom I never met in the natural world), I kept hearing that same still, small voice saying, "Include the prophetic dream of Nipsey Hussle in the book." So, I perceived that the Holy Spirit was speaking to me and possibly trying to send a subtle message and/or warning to all of those whom Nipsey loved. So, for that reason, I have included the prophetic dream of Nipsey Hussle in this book.

He was more than just a man who lived and walked the

earth; he was a hero to the downtrodden, drug addict, street sweeper, shoeshine man, and poor pauper in the hood.

He was a hidden genius who pulled himself out of a gutter hole in the wall and succeeded in making it out of the hood. Thus, he became my hero too.

I do believe this section of the book and the dream itself will be received with some level of controversy, and understandably so, for this is a natural phenomenon of the world we live in today. However, I am also aware that the entire book itself will be received with some level of controversy and varying degrees of opinions and ideas. However, in the spirit of Nipsey Hussle, I will say to those of you who may be angry and/or in disbelief of the contents of the dream and/or this book that I know, and Nipsey knows you love him deeply and will love him for the remainder of your natural lives and beyond for those of you who make it to the light. You will meet him again in paradise.

The prophetic symbolic dream of Nipsey Hussle, Tha Great, came eleven days before his death. Date of the dream: Wednesday, March 20, 2019.

Title of Dream: "Prophetic Nightmare"

Part One

When I awoke from this dream, I was in a super sweat,

and it was sort of violently. I was swinging my arms as if I was trying to fight my way out of the dream so that I could wake up from it. It was scary; it was a nightmare.

This dream was filled with chaos. It was more like multiple scattered dreams in one. I felt like I was all over the place. The only two parts of the dream that I can remember are written below.

In one of the dreams, I was in a room, and a small daddy-longlegs spider crawled out of a small vent in a wall. The kind of vents you see on the floors in older model homes. Once out of the vent, the spider did not look small at all. It looked more like a big daddy-longlegs spider with extremely long legs. The spider also had a long tail trailing behind it. The tail looked like a peacock's tail, the way a peacock's tail looks when it closes its feathers behind the back of its body. The spider had the appearance of a king with the regalia of royalty. It was trimmed in gold on its entire body (arms and legs). It wore a crown on its head and had the appearance of a king. Once it was fully out of the vent, it stood upright and began walking like a man, like a distinguished dignitary or man of royalty. It held its head up high and almost appeared to have the face of a man. It wore a long red velvet robe with white fur trimmings. There were small black dots on the white fur trimming. The rob was like the ones worn by kings in the eighteenth century. The spider was grayish or whitish in color. It was definitely not your typical spider. It felt more like it was a human being or a human man. It had multiple legs like a typical daddy-longlegs spider.

At first, I wasn't sure if it was a deadly spider or something else. But within seconds, I became fully aware that it was not your typical spider and that it was deadly. Hence, ready for a fight. It felt like it was fighting to protect something or to exert power. As the spider faced me, it began walking toward me. It looked me straight in the face as it approached me, and I became desperately afraid. So, I began fighting with it. But it was no easy fight. I had to fight it with excessive force to destroy it, which eventually I did. But again, it was not easy to destroy because it put up a good fight as if it knew it was fighting for its life. "It" meaning the daddy-longlegs spider with the long peacock tail hanging in its rear. It took me several attempts of swinging my weapon to destroy it before it would succumb to annihilation.

Thus, it took me several attempts of swinging whatever I was holding in my hands to finally break it into pieces and destroy it. Note: I could not see what I was holding in my hands; I could only feel that I was swinging something very forcefully. The spider was extremely difficult to destroy and was only defeated by being broken into several pieces.

Keep in mind I did not know Nipsey before he died and had never met him prior to his death on March 31, 2019.

The only time I had ever seen Nipsey prior to his death was when he and his wife, Lauren, were sitting next to each other at the Grammy Awards in January 2019. I caught a very brief glimpse of him.

Part Two

The second part of the dream was a bit sketchy and hard to remember. All I can remember about this part of the dream is being in a dark dingy-looking place that resembled a large warehouse. There were other people standing around in there. I remember the people appeared to be all males. According to the demon or monstrous being, one of the males had committed suicide; I am not sure how recent the suicide was. After being in the warehouse (very briefly), I somehow ended up outside and was away from the rest of the people, males, still inside the dark, dingy warehouse. Within moments of being outside, a monstrous-looking thing came out of nowhere and stood in front of me. It or he began speaking to me. It said, in a very deep raspy voice, "Speaking of the gentleman who committed suicide, I have him already. I have three more to get." When he said he had three more to get, he was speaking of three other males inside the warehouse. The men in the warehouse were committing sin. The men appeared to be African American, but I did not make a note of their ethnicity on the scratch paper when I awoke from the dream. They, meaning the men inside the large warehouse, were many. A large group of males was standing inside the dark, dingy warehouse building.

The Appearance of the Monstrous Being

My vision of the monstrous being is as follows: it was a very slender, hairless creature that stood tall and upright like a human being or a man. Its color was deep dark grayish-black (dingy). I could not see its eyes or any real facial features. I am not sure it had facial features. I was too afraid to look. Its voice was deep, very deep, and raspy.

After the monstrous being finished speaking to me, I turned and ran away from it. I ran back into the warehouse where all the males were standing around. I tried to tell them what I had just experienced. I told them exactly what the demon, monstrous thing, had said to me: "I have one already, and I have three more to get." After I told them the words the demon had spoken, I awoke from the dream.

The Timeline:

Prophetic dream of the Nipsey spider: March 20, 2019 (eleven days before his death).

Nipsey died: March 31, 2019 (eleven days after the dream).

Nipsey's funeral was held: April 11, 2019 (eleven days

after his death).

Nipsey was buried: April 12, 2019 (twelve days after his death).

The meaning of the number eleven in the Hebrew Bible: 12 − 1 = disorganization, incomplete, lack, or 10 + 1 = excess (both signify imperfection), transition (moving back to ten or ahead moving forward to twelve), betrayal, idolatry, bribery, and rebellion to heavenly authority. The number eleven is usually about doing what is right in your own eyes. Its action is based on "what I feel," not "what is written." Thus, the number eleven is highly associated with the spirit of the anti-Christ.

The meaning of the number twelve in the Hebrew Bible: Perfect government, order, organization, and unity.

$3 \times 4 = 12$

Again, looking at the ideal for numbers three and four, we can see that when the seed is ripened (three) ("three" means "ripened") with the Holy Spirit (four) (four represents the Holy Spirit), it produces resurrection life (three also represents resurrection life), that is powered by the divine government (four also represents divine government).

The above timeline seems to illustrate that Nipsey transitioned from self-love and self-orientation to God-love and God-orientation and became ripened and conjoined with the divine Holy Spirit when he transitioned.

Song number twelve on *Victory Lap* is titled "Million While You Young."

Song number sixteen, the last song on *Victory Lap*, is titled "Right Hand to God."

Please note: 12 + 4 (four represents the Holy Spirit) = 16. Sixteen, the last song, symbolizes the end of the journey for Nipsey, who raised his right hand to ascend to heaven to live in paradise with his Lord and Savior.

My Interpretation of the Hidden Message in the Timeline:

Hence, the young millionaire moved from imperfect self-love to perfect love for God and became conjoined with the Holy Spirit during his transition from self-love and idolatry to God-love and family. The Holy Spirit heard his prayers and saw him through the journey. When Nipsey was fully ripened (enlightened), the Holy Spirit took him to be with God in heaven. It is my opinion that God had shown him mercy, grace, and favor.

Nipsey Hussle's funeral included music and tears as he was sent off like a king.

Oh, one last thing...the day of Nipsey's funeral, I was at a place where Nipsey held his first job: Chambers Shoeshine. We were all participating in the procession as it passed, carrying Nipsey's body to its final resting place, and a little girl wearing a white T-shirt with a rainbow-colored unicorn on it walked up to me and said, "Are you Nipsey Hussle's friend?" Tears came to my eyes as I looked at her and responded, "We are all Nipsey Hussle's friends, and so are you."

Rihanna, "I'm Not Trash"

"They thought I was trash. Now they know I wasn't."
March 8, 2022

Was it by chance or happenstance that she and I would meet the same week that my review of the final edits for this book was due to be sent to the publisher? I'll let you decide that for yourselves.

One late afternoon she strolled into my office with all the innocence and beauty of an eight-year-old child. At first sight, she looked like a perfectly normal and happy little girl. Well, that is, until we began the child interview.

"Hi, Rihanna, I am going to ask you a few questions." So, I began the interview as I typically would by asking, "Who do you live with?" and "What do you like to do after school?"

And without any further prompting, Rihanna replied, "I live with my good mom. I used to live with my bad mom, but now I live with my good mom."

She didn't stop talking, so I sat in silence and continued to listen. After a few minutes, I interjected and asked, "Your bad mom? You have a bad mom?"

She replied, "Yes, my bad mom, well, I mean my evil mom. She used to punch me. She was evil, and I am happy I live with my good mom now."

As you can probably imagine, I sat looking at her in absolute surprise and awe as she spoke. I was astounded to hear her speak so candidly about her feelings, especially to an adult she had just met five minutes before. I have never in my entire career as a psychologist heard a child of this age refer to their mothers in such a manner and with such conviction. Typically, very young children don't really understand how to express their pain or emotional trauma. But Rihanna did, much like an older child would.

Immediately after my meeting with Rihanna ended, I called her home. I had to get some answers and needed those answers right away. Upon speaking to the woman who answered the phone, I discovered that Rihanna had been adopted and taken away from her biological mother at birth. She was currently residing with her second set of parents (her adopted mom). The very moment Rihanna exited her mother's womb, she was rushed into critical care for infants. She and her biological mother never met again.

So, of course, at this point in the conversation, I was very confused. I began to question the adoptive mother about the course of Rihanna's life immediately after being released from the hospital. And she explained that Rihanna had initially been placed with a local foster family that had expressed an interest in raising her as their child. However, while Rihanna was still just a one-year-old infant, the first foster family discovered that Rihanna was not actually Latino but was part Latino and part African American. Her biological father was African American. Shortly after discovering this, they rejected her and returned her to child protective services (DCFS). The family was a local Latino family.

After being returned to the foster care system and presumably placed in a waiting facility, she was selected by a new foster family, which became her current adoptive family. *Oh, okay, so that makes sense: her first foster mom punched her*, I thought.

But after I revealed to Rihanna's new adoptive mom what Rihanna had told me about her two moms, she asked, "How did she know that?"

I replied, "How did she know what?"

She said, "That her mother punched her." She went on to explain why Rihanna never actually met her biological mother. She said that it had been discovered that Rihanna's biological mother had attempted to self-abort on several occasions by punching herself in the stomach repeatedly. Rihanna's dad has never been seen or heard of at all, even after DCFS completed a nationwide search to try to find and identify him.

Of course, I could not believe what I was hearing. My heart was aching for this poor child, who had survived a botched-attempted abortion just seven years prior to our first meeting. But before you rush to judgment about her biological "evil mom," I think you should know that Rihanna's biological mother is diagnosed as intellectually disabled (mild mental retardation). That said, I discovered that Rihanna also has several disabling conditions as a result of being punched while still developing in her mother's womb. But one thing appears to have remained intact: yes, you guessed it, her memory (albeit supernaturally). I call it a powerful supernatural miracle because she could still remember the pain that she had experienced while developing in her mother's womb. She had an absolute awareness of what was happening to her, and she didn't use ambiguous words to describe what she felt, like "beat" or "hit." She used the exact word for what she was feeling, "punched." How did she know to use the word "punched"? And how did she know how to express a deeper, more painful emotion by not only referring to her biological mother as "bad" but also referring to her as "evil"? The word "evil" adds an extra emphasis to express the devastating pain and emotions that she experienced while developing in her mother's womb and the pain she continues to feel to this day.

Rihanna's adoptive mom indicated Rihanna was never told about the abuse or her natural mother. She has never been told that her natural mother abused her or was bad or evil. So, how did she know she had been punched by her natural mother while she was still developing in the womb? Who told her, or how did she remember? There's only one answer (well, at least for me): God.

She was alive in the womb from start to finish and could hear and feel everything her mother was saying and doing to her. Does this not solidify the fact that babies in the womb (no matter the developmental age) are just as human as you and me and experience a range of emotions just like you and me?

I am astonished beyond belief. I have never in my career heard a seven-year-old child (with such severe developmental cognitive delays) use the word "evil," not before or since meeting Rihanna. And please note: "evil" is a word that Rihanna still cannot even read due to her developmental delays. I hope, one day, you get to meet this truly special miracle child (God's little princess), a living survivor of a failed-attempt abortion in her mother's womb.

And finally…

Why now? Why did I meet her now? The same year, the same month, and the same week of final edits for the book, just before publishing?

BIBLIOGRAPHY

"The Meaning of Numbers: The Number 22" Biblestudy. org. Accessed February 2, 2022. https://www. biblestudy.org/bibleref/meaning-of-numbers-in-bible/22.html.

"Time's arrow: Albert Einstein's letters to Michele Besso." November 14, 2017. https://www.christies. com/features/Einstein-letters-to-Michele-Besso-8422-1.aspx.

Bryant, Dorothy. *The Kin of Ata Are Waiting for You.* New York, NY: Random House Publishing Group, 2010. books.google.com/books?id=1EHmJ5VF-wx4C.

Burton, Tim, dir. *Dark Shadows*. 2012. Movie. https:// www.imdb.com/title/tt1077368.

De Vorzon, Barry and Perry L Botkin. Carpenters. "Bless the Beast and the Children." Track 7 on *A Song for You.* © Sony/ATV Music Publishing LLC. https://genius.com/Carpenters-bless-the-beasts-and-the-children-lyrics.

Friedman, Manis. "Love, Love, Love, Love, Love, What Is Love?" YouTube video. December 18, 2021. https://youtu.be/YgtjI7ebXVs.

Friedman, Manis. "The Soul and Its Life." YouTube video. October 26, 2021. https://youtu.be/m_9zkewfT10.

LoveIsrael.org with Baruch Korman "Exodus, chapter 21, part 2." YouTube video. March 29, 2020. https://www.youtube.com/watch?v=D_VmQppBTD8.

LoveIsrael.org with Baruch Korman "God's Judgement upon Babylon?" YouTube video. October 16, 2021. https://www.youtube.com/watch?v=tC-cU1XnEmig.

Page, George and Thomas Lovejoy. *Nature*. 1982–. TV series. https://www.imdb.com/title/tt0083452/?ref_=fn_al_tt_2.

Schneider, K. A. *Discovering the Jewish Jesus*. Quoted on Daystar Television Network. August 2019.

Shane, Philip, dir. *Einstein*. 2008. TV movie. https://www.imdb.com/title/tt1334528.

ABOUT THE AUTHOR

Taylor Coco Rochelle Patterson is a devoted follower of Jesus Christ, whom she accepted as her Lord and Savior as a young child. She is an alumnus of the University of California, Los Angeles (UCLA), school psychologist, adjunct professor, and Zumba dancer. She also has a background in acting and creative arts. This book was written to be a light to the world and to give a voice to aborted children.

Taylor grew up in Oakland, California, where she narrowly escaped becoming a high school dropout due to becoming pregnant as a teenager. Her strong Christian mother (Valerie) refused to let her have an abortion; thus, she became a single teenage mother. During the time, Taylor continued to be pro-choice and a staunch advocate for abortion and women's choice. She remained a pro-choice advocate until 2012 when Jesus and the Holy Spirit descended upon her life with a heart-crushing revelation that would change her life forever and turn her heart of stone into a heart for God.

If given the choice of their voice on the earth, they would whisper, "Mommy, can I live in heaven? Mommy, I love you always."

Refer to the Instagram account @godsanswertoabortion.